Siddhartha Reimagined

Also from EATMS Productions

Books on power, survival, women's autonomy, and the systems shaping modern America.

Nonfiction

Billionaires, Capitalism, and Power

Evil and the Mountain Ungreed
Self Help for American Billionaires
Selfish Steve and the Ivory Tower
Tariffs, Taxes, & Face-Eating Leopards
Ban Billionaires: Fascism Fix

Fascism, Religion, and Cultural Control

Self Help for the Manosphere
Fascism 2025
Fascism & the Perverts & the Greed Virus
Christian Fascism Marriage Book
Tyranny, Table Manners, & Tiramisu

Guides for Women's Autonomy and Protection

How to Survive in Post-America as a Woman
Project 2025 American Drag
4B – Burn, Ban, Boycott, Build
4B OG – So No Go GYN
I'm Glad He's Dead

Analysis of Authoritarian Project 2025

Project 2025: The Blueprint
Project 2025: The List
Project 2025, Christian Dumb Dumbs, & The Republican Agenda
Fascism, Project 2025, & The Pinkprint

Modern Rewrites for Women

Stoic Principles Reimagined
Siddhartha Reimagined
The Prince Reimagined for Women
The Art of War Reimagined for Women
The Jungle Reimagined
The Constitution Reimagined for Women

Machine Learning Series

AI, Bitcoin, Nostr for Women
AI, Safety, & Security for Women
AI, Anxiety, & Health for Women
AI, Kids, & Family Safety for Women
AI, Creativity, & Personal Expression for Women
AI, Independent Work, & Parallel Power for Women

Social Systems Series

Emotional Labor for Women
Household Power for Women
Workplace Power for Women
Medical Bias for Women
Aging Systems for Women
Recovery Systems for Women

Fiction

Dystopian Stories of Resistance and Collapse

Propaganda Paige & the Missing Prosperity
Propaganda Paige & the TIDE Manifesto
Propaganda Paige & the Shadow Cartographers
Propaganda Paige & the Prosperity Alliance
Propaganda Paige & the Shattered Truth
Propaganda Paige & the Rising TIDE
Propaganda Paige & the Last Bastion
Propaganda Paige & the Dawn of Prosperity
Project 2025: Dorian — The Last Men
Project 2025: Boy — A Last Men Novel

Siddhartha Reimagined for Modern Challenges

Sympathy & Support 1

Inspired by Herman Hesse's Original Version of Siddhartha

by
Esme Mees
& Claudia Mayfair

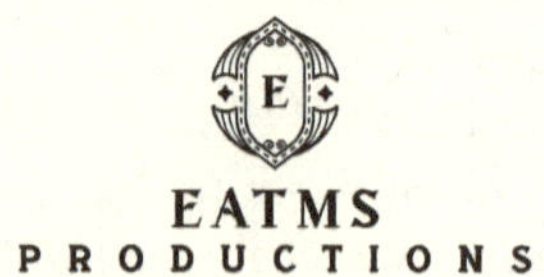

This title is part of an ongoing body of work. All EATMS Productions titles, across all series, authors, and formats, are components of a single connected project.

This book is a work of opinion and creative interpretation. While some names and events may be referenced or alluded to, any claims made are based on publicly available information and are intended as satire, parody, or commentary on societal and political issues. The content should not be interpreted as factual assertions about any individual or entity. The author does not intend to defraud, defame, or mislead, and encourages readers to form their own conclusions. Any resemblance to real persons, living or dead, is purely coincidental unless explicitly noted otherwise.

ISBN 978-1-966014-95-9

Cover, interior design, interior prints by: Esme Mees

eatms@pm.me
www.eatms.me

Printed in the United States of America.

You, Venerable One, may indeed be a seeker, for, striving toward your goal, there is much you do not see which is right before your eyes.

— Herman Hesse, *Siddhartha*

Table of Contents

Introduction

Nobody is Coming to Save You

There are stories so ancient and so profound that they become part of the landscape of human thought, their wisdom carried like a river winding through generations, sometimes silent, sometimes roaring. *Siddhartha* is one such story. Herman Hesse's meditation on enlightenment, self-discovery, and the winding paths that lead to wisdom has endured because it speaks to the universal and the eternal. And yet, for all its insight, there are cracks in its narrative that modernity exposes, questions it does not ask, perspectives it does not fully embrace.

The world has changed since Hesse's time, and the challenges we face now demand a reimagining of the path to self-actualization. Today's seeker is not wandering through ancient India but navigating an era defined by new and old injustices: consumerism, climate crisis, patriarchy, racism, bigotry, and economic disparity. In a world where spirituality is often commodified, where the weight of systems and institutions presses heavily upon the individual, the journey to truth is less about solitude and more about interconnected struggle.

To reimagine *Siddhartha* is not to discard its wisdom, but to acknowledge the voices that were absent, the perspectives that were overlooked, and the struggles that define our age. In this version, our seeker is not a prince of privilege stepping away from excess, but a woman born into a world that never presumed to place a crown upon her head. Her path is not one of renouncing what she has, but of claiming what she was never granted.

She is raised in the corridors of power, among those who justify oppression with faith and who wield wealth as though it were divine right. She learns the language of control before she learns the language of freedom. And yet, from the beginning, she senses something hollow in the world she is told to accept. The contradictions press against her consciousness, sermons on humility spoken from gilded pulpits, prayers for the poor uttered by those who keep their gates locked against them.

Her journey is not one of comfort or ease. The road to self-knowledge is no gentle river but a sea roiling with tyranny, the tide of history pulling in currents of greed, violence, and erasure. She does not seek enlightenment as a retreat from the world, but as a confrontation with it. She walks through the centers of power and the margins of society, listening, unlearning, and relearning. She meets those whose wisdom is not written in sacred texts but carved into the lines of their hands, the callouses of their labor, the poetry of their opposition.

Like Hesse's *Siddhartha*, she is driven by an insatiable need to understand. But where his journey led him to solitary contemplation, hers is shaped by the undeniable fact that the self does not exist in isolation. In a world of interwoven systems and collective struggles, individual enlightenment is insufficient. Her awakening is not a quiet retreat into nature, but an active refusal to accept a world where suffering is deemed inevitable.

She learns from revolutionaries and caretakers, from the voices ignored by history. She is shaped by those who have been dismissed as unworthy of wisdom, women, the working class, the displaced, the unheard. And in their stories, she finds the deepest truths, not about a path to transcend suffering, but about a way to live within it, to fight against it, to create something beyond it.

This reimagining of *Siddhartha* is not an abandonment of its original intent but a deepening of its inquiry. What does it mean to seek truth in a world built on falsehoods? How does one find wisdom when knowledge is hoarded by the powerful? What does enlightenment look like when the road to it is blocked by borders, by barriers, by those who would rather maintain control than allow others to awaken?

In every age, there are seekers, women and men whose hunger for truth and meaning will not be satisfied by the dogma of their predecessors. They are born into a world that expects their unquestioning compliance, a world that has its answers pre-packaged, its systems solidified, and its gods already enthroned. But the seekers are restless. They are troubled by what others take for granted, and what should be enough for them, security, tradition, a well-trodden path, becomes the very weight that presses upon their souls. They long for something more than inherited wisdom; they yearn to carve a path of their own.

Silvia, as she is known in this reimagining, is one such seeker. Her journey is not merely of rebellion, but of profound transformation, a pilgrimage that leads her through the illusions of power, wealth, pleasure, and even asceticism, only to arrive at a truth that cannot be given to her but must be earned. The tale has endured because the search for meaning is an eternal endeavor, one that transcends geography and time. And yet, the world of *Siddhartha* is not our world. The spiritual crises of the past were not complicated by the relentless noise of modernity, the insidious pull of capitalism, the commodification of wisdom itself. To seek truth today is to do so amidst a deluge of distractions, misinformation, and systems designed to keep the soul in a state of perpetual restlessness.

This reimagining of *Siddhartha* is not a mere retelling; it is an urgent adaptation, one that grapples with the spiritual and existential dilemmas of our own age. The Silvia of this story is not a princess in a palace but the daughter of privilege in a world where wealth consolidates into fewer hands and inequality stretches ever wider. She is raised in a home of ideological certainties, where the gods are economic systems, and faith is placed not in divine grace but in the power of the market, the inevitability of progress, the sanctity of ownership. From birth, she is trained to inherit the machinery of control, to wield influence with the assuredness of those who have never been made to question their right to rule.

Like the *Siddhartha* of old, she does what no one in her world expects, she walks away. Not in a romanticized escape but in a slow, painful severing, in the terrifying realization that the world outside her privilege is not simply a place of suffering but a place where she, for the first time, must learn to exist without the safety of power.

This is not a story that offers easy resolutions. It does not seek to provide the comfort of closure or the assurance that every seeker will find what they are looking for. It is, instead, an invitation, to step away from certainty, to question not only the world but oneself, to accept that the path is neither clear nor linear. It is for those who suspect that the greatest lie ever told is that the world is already known, that all questions have been answered. It is for those who, despite everything, still long to seek.

To those who are restless, to those who find no peace in the hollow comforts offered by modern life, to those who refuse to accept the narratives handed down to them, this story is for you. The road ahead is uncertain, but it is yours to walk.

Esme Mees & Claudia Mayfair, Winter 2025

Chapter 1

Family, Religion, Greed, and Power

From the moment Silvia could form a thought of her own, she understood that power was both a birthright and a performance, a stage upon which the Arnolds played their parts with unwavering conviction. Theirs was a house of polished surfaces, mahogany staircases and chandeliers whose crystals shimmered like fallen stars, but beneath its grand exterior lay a foundation built not on piety, as was so often proclaimed, but on an inheritance of avarice. Her father, Senator Ben Arnold, was a man who knew how to bend language to his will, how to weave scripture into a net that ensnared both the faithful and the desperate. He spoke of duty and providence, of God's plan for leadership, and in doing so, he made their wealth seem less an accident of birth than a divine appointment.

Her mother, Nancy Arnold, had a devotion that was, in its own way, even more ruthless. She was a woman whose prayers carried the weight of command, whose charity never failed to include photographers. It was she who presided over the great and ostentatious luncheons where the city's wealthiest gathered to discuss, with feigned gravity, the plight of the less fortunate. She wore humility like a garment woven from the finest silk, a careful arrangement of modesty and grace that only enhanced the splendor of her position. The poor were, for her, an abstract problem to be discussed in theoretical terms over gilded plates of delicacies, their suffering distant and malleable, to be shaped into whatever narrative best suited her influence.

As a child, Silvia had been slow to recognize the contradictions embedded in their world, for the stories she was told were of sacrifice and service, of a family ordained to guide the weak and ignorant toward the light. But as she grew, she began to see not only the chasms between word and deed, but also the quiet, unacknowledged violence in the structure of their lives.

She saw it in the hunched backs of the gardeners, who were invisible until the moment their work was deemed unsatisfactory. She saw it in the downcast eyes of the maids, who disappeared into the shadows when guests arrived, as if the very hands that scrubbed the floors and carried the silver trays must not be allowed to exist in the same light as those they served. She saw it in the way her mother's charities never extended to the staff, who were expected to be grateful for the privilege of employment.

Her father's voice, so practiced in the halls of government, was just as persuasive within the walls of their home. At dinner, he spoke of policy in tones of great moral authority, expounding on the necessity of economic discipline, of incentives, of the natural order of society. "The world," he would say, with the air of a man revealing a secret of profound importance, "divides itself into those who lead and those who follow. This is not cruelty, my dear, it is wisdom. It is the very nature of things." And with a satisfied nod, he would return to his meal, carving into the tender flesh of a lamb whose sacrifice, unlike so many others, was acknowledged only in the silence that followed.

Silvia listened. She listened and she watched, and as she grew older, she found herself unable to reconcile the warm timbre of her father's voice with the hard glint in his eyes when he spoke of the poor as an inconvenience, an obstacle to be managed rather than a people to be served. She found herself questioning the insistence that their position was a matter of divine will when she saw, with each passing year, the increasing desperation of those who lived beyond the high walls of their estate. She found herself wondering what sort of God would ordain the suffering of so many for the comfort of so few.

The first time she voiced her doubts, it was to her mother, who sat at her vanity, her fingers carefully fastening an emerald brooch at the collar of her silk blouse. "Mother," Silvia had said, hesitantly, "if we are meant to help the poor, why do we live in a house so grand?"

Her mother's hands stilled for only a moment before she turned, her expression a mixture of indulgence and amusement. "My dear girl," she said, smoothing a stray curl from Silvia's brow, "the Lord blesses those who are worthy. It is our duty to guide those less fortunate, not to reduce ourselves to their station. To lead, one must be above. That is the order of things."

It was a lesson repeated often, with varying degrees of gentleness. When Silvia suggested that perhaps they might do more, perhaps the grand dinners might serve the hungry rather than the already satisfied, her father laughed and called her sentimental. "The world is not changed by feeling, Silvia. It is changed by power. And power," he added, pressing a firm hand to her shoulder, "is not given. It is taken, maintained, and wielded with wisdom."

Yet Silvia could not quiet the discord that grew within her. The more she learned of their world, the more she saw the ways in which wealth was a fortress, one built not merely to preserve comfort but to exclude those who did not belong. The teachings of her father, the doctrine of her mother, had been constructed with the same precision as the high walls of their estate, and she had been expected to live within them, to accept their truth as immutable. But she could not.

The first real act of defiance came not in words but in silence. At one of her mother's charity galas, as the room filled with laughter and clinking glasses, Silvia stood apart, watching as figures draped in finery spoke of the plight of the unfortunate while sipping champagne imported from across the sea. Her father delivered a speech that evening, one of his finest, full of carefully measured words about duty and faith, about the necessity of discipline and the virtue of the free market. He ended, as he so often did, with a verse from scripture, a polished gem of rhetoric that left his audience nodding in reverent agreement. But as the applause swelled around her, Silvia did not clap.

That night, as she lay in bed, the weight of her father's words pressing against her chest like a heavy stone, she stared at the ceiling and whispered a single question into the darkness. "What if they are wrong?"

It was the beginning of something, something that could not yet be named, something as vast and uncertain as the night sky beyond her window. But even as she closed her eyes, she knew this much: she would not inherit their world without question. She would not accept their power as a gift from God. She would not be another voice in the chorus of self-righteousness that echoed through their halls. She would listen. And she would wait. And one day, when the time was right, she would speak.

Silvia's Academic Leadership

Silvia's intellect was a thing of early and evident distinction, a force as undeniable as the seasons shifting or the river cutting its determined course through the land. From the time she was a child, her mind absorbed knowledge with a hunger that exceeded mere precocity; it was as if she was called to it, as if learning itself had chosen her as its vessel. Her father, ever the calculating statesman, saw in her the makings of an orator, a leader who might one day wield her intellect with as much deftness as he wielded his silver tongue. Her mother, equally ambitious but more invested in the spectacle of piety, envisioned Silvia as the luminous embodiment of their family's divine favor, a testament to God's grace and the unimpeachable rightness of their station.

To cultivate her gifts, no expense was spared. Tutors arrived daily at their grand estate, solemn figures who introduced her to Latin declensions before she had outgrown the nursery, who drilled her in the histories of conquests and kings while she still wore ribbons in her hair. She was placed in the most exclusive schools, among peers who bore names of old renown, the sons and daughters of power. Yet even among such privileged company, Silvia shone. She devoured texts with an insatiable appetite, mastering subjects with an ease that alarmed and delighted her parents in equal measure.

Yet for all her learning, there was a danger in Silvia's education, one that neither of her parents had anticipated, nor could they have controlled had they foreseen it. The more she studied, the more she questioned, and the more she questioned, the more uneasy she became. It was one thing to memorize the axioms of governance, to recite the virtues of discipline and authority as they had been handed down for centuries; it was quite another to sit with the accounts of those who had suffered under those very systems, who had been ground beneath the boots of those in power, who had risen, bloodied but unbowed, to demand their share of the world's justice.

History lessons that were meant to reinforce the grandeur of empire instead stirred in Silvia a deep unease. The names of the great leaders and visionaries that her teachers extolled as paragons of governance, those who had subdued foreign lands, consolidated power, or bent the economy to their will, began to appear in a different light. She saw not the triumphs of civilization, but the tally of human suffering left in their wake. In the quiet solitude of the library, she traced the patterns of uprisings, of revolutions led by those deemed lesser, only to realize that they were not lesser in the way that power dictated, but only in the way that history had chosen to remember them.

Literature, too, became a source of friction. She found herself drawn not to the polished narratives of conquest or the moralistic tales meant to guide young minds toward virtue, but to the works that questioned the very fabric of her world. She read, in hushed defiance, the works of authors who had dared to expose the hypocrisies of their time, who had carved out stories of women and men who defied the order imposed upon them. With every page turned, Silvia felt her foundation tremble. How many of these stories were whispered truths masquerading as fiction? How many of the villains bore the same cold smile as her father, the same calculating gaze as the men who dined at their table, their words dripping with civility even as they dictated policies that sentenced the poor to further deprivation?

Theology, that cornerstone upon which her family had constructed their legitimacy, soon became a battleground in her mind. She had been raised to accept the divine order of things, to believe that their wealth was a reflection of God's blessing, that power was merely the righteous man's due. But when she studied the scripture without the guiding hand of her father's interpretations, she found, buried beneath layers of doctrine, a faith that did not resemble the one she had been taught.

She saw, in the teachings of Christ, not a champion of power but a voice raised for the downtrodden. She read of a man who walked among the poor, who cast scorn upon the wealthy, who overturned the tables of the moneychangers, who told the rich to relinquish their wealth if they wished to enter the kingdom of heaven. And yet, how often had her father invoked this very man's name in the halls of government while drafting policies that cut aid to the desperate? How often had her mother, with her angelic smile and diamond-encrusted cross, turned away from the pleading eyes of those who served in their home, dismissing their concerns as the natural order of things?

Silvia had once believed in her family's version of faith, but now she saw it for what it was, a tool, a means of control wielded with precision and without remorse. The God her parents worshipped was not the one of scripture, but one of convenience, one who justified their privilege and soothed their conscience. The realization settled over her not with the clarity of a single moment, but as a slow and creeping tide, rising with each contradiction she uncovered, with each truth that gnawed at the foundation of her upbringing.

For a time, Silvia kept her doubts to herself. She moved through the motions of her education with the same discipline, the same outward enthusiasm, careful not to betray the growing fissures in her belief. But her silence was not one of resignation, it was one of strategy. She understood, as she had been taught, the value of patience. She knew that to challenge her father directly, to confront her mother with her doubts, would be to invite a storm she was not yet prepared to weather. So she waited, absorbing all she could, honing the sharp edges of her mind into weapons she would one day wield in her own battle against the falsehoods that had shaped her childhood.

It was in the quiet of her study, late at night when the house was still, that she laid the foundation of her own awakening. She read texts that her father would have deemed subversive, philosophies that questioned the very structures upon which her family's power rested. She began to write, not yet with the intent to share, but to understand herself. Her journals became filled with questions that had no simple answers, thoughts that pushed against the boundaries of what she had been told was true. And yet, for all the uncertainty, there was exhilaration in the discovery.

Her parents continued to believe they were shaping her for greatness, crafting her into the perfect heir to their legacy. They mistook her quiet compliance for acceptance, her disciplined studies for devotion. They did not see the slow unraveling that was taking place within her, did not recognize the shift in her eyes when she looked upon the portraits of her ancestors, those men and women who had built their fortune on the labor of others.

They had raised her to lead, and perhaps, in the end, they had been successful, but they had never considered what direction she might choose to take. She would lead, yes, but not as they had envisioned. The road ahead was uncertain, its destination unclear, but Silvia was no longer afraid of uncertainty. In fact, she welcomed it. The world her parents had built was one of rigid lines and predetermined paths, but she had glimpsed something beyond those confines, something wild and free and utterly irreconcilable with the narrow life they had planned for her.

And so, she continued her studies, playing the role of the obedient daughter, the bright and promising scholar, all the while carrying the quiet revolution within her, waiting for the day when she would no longer have to pretend.

Conversations with Maya

Maya had always been Silvia's counterweight, the force that kept her tethered to the ground when the opulence of her upbringing threatened to carry her away into complacency. Their friendship had grown in the corners of gilded rooms and garden terraces, in whispered confidences exchanged between the formalities imposed upon them. Silvia's world had always been one of polished surfaces and well-rehearsed pieties, where charity was a spectacle and righteousness a performance. Maya, sharp-eyed and sharper-tongued, was the first person who had ever dared to point out the cracks in that veneer.

One evening, as they sat beneath the shadow of the grand estate where Silvia had spent her childhood, Maya spoke words that Silvia had long feared to say aloud. "Do you ever wonder," she asked, tilting her head toward the sky, "if all of this is just a lie?"

Silvia traced the outline of a constellation, the stars struggling to shine through the light pollution of the city. "What do you mean?" she asked, though she already knew.

"I mean," Maya continued, leaning forward with the urgency of someone who had been waiting for this moment, "your family talks about God and justice, but what do they actually do? They throw money at problems, but they never solve them. They preach about equality, but they live in a mansion while people starve in the streets. How can you stand it?"

The words struck Silvia with the force of a blow, not because they were new, but because they were true. She had thought them a thousand times, but there was a power in hearing them spoken, in having them reflected back at her in Maya's unwavering gaze.

"I don't know," she admitted at last, her voice barely above a whisper. "I don't know how to reconcile it."

Maya sighed, reclining against the cool stone of the garden wall. "You don't have to reconcile it," she said. "You just have to see it for what it is."

Silvia knew Maya's perspective had been shaped by her father, a journalist whose work had cost him friendships and, at times, security. Unlike the men who visited the Arnold estate, expounding on the virtues of wealth while sipping fine wine, Maya's father had built his career on exposing the abuses of the powerful. He had taught her to see past the façade, to question everything, to refuse to be dazzled by displays of grandeur.

Silvia, despite all her education, had never been taught to question. She had been raised to believe in the righteousness of her family's position, in the natural order of things. Yet, the contradictions Maya pointed out were becoming harder to ignore.

She thought of the charity galas her mother organized, events where guests congratulated themselves for their generosity while dining on extravagant meals. She thought of the carefully curated speeches her father delivered on justice and responsibility, words that rang hollow against the backdrop of their sprawling estate. And she thought of the people outside their gates, unseen and unheard, whose struggles were neatly reduced to statistics in policy discussions.
Maya picked up a stone and tossed it idly between her hands. "You ever notice how your father never really answers questions?"

Silvia frowned. "What do you mean?"

"He talks a lot," Maya said, "but it's never an answer. It's all rhetoric. He could say something that sounds profound, but if you actually listen, it's just a way of maintaining the status quo."

Silvia thought back to her father's speeches, the way he spoke with conviction, the way he made the most harmful policies seem reasonable, even necessary. "You think he knows?" she asked. "That it's all just... words?"

Maya shrugged. "Maybe. Or maybe he believes it. That's the thing about power, it convinces you that you deserve it."

Silvia wanted to argue, to defend the father she loved, but she couldn't. Not when the evidence of his hypocrisy was written across every decision he made. Instead, she asked, "And what about us? We've benefited from it, too."

Maya turned to her, her expression unreadable. "Yeah," she said. "And that's why we have to be the ones to break it."

The idea of breaking anything in her world was foreign to Silvia. She had been taught to uphold, to maintain, to preserve. Yet, as she looked around the grand estate, the carefully cultivated gardens, the towering columns that loomed over them, she wondered if the world she had inherited was worth preserving at all.

Maya was relentless in her observations, pointing out things that Silvia had trained herself to ignore. When they walked through the city together, Maya saw the people Silvia had been raised to overlook, the workers in the kitchens of the restaurants they dined in, the security guards stationed at the doors of high-end shops, the janitors cleaning the polished floors of her father's office building long after the executives had left for the night.

"These are the people who actually keep the world running," Maya said once as they stood on a busy street corner. "Not the politicians, not the bankers, not the CEOs. Without them, everything collapses. And yet, we act like they're invisible."

Silvia wanted to argue, to say that her family's work was important too, but the words felt thin, insubstantial. She had spent years convincing herself that wealth and power could be wielded for good, but the cracks in that belief were widening, and Maya's words were the hammer chipping away at what remained.

It wasn't that Silvia had never questioned before; she had. But questions in solitude could be rationalized away, could be silenced by duty and expectation. Maya was relentless, refusing to let her retreat into comfortable ignorance.

One night, after another of their long discussions, Silvia lay awake in bed, staring at the ornate ceiling of her room. For the first time, she allowed herself to fully acknowledge what she had long suspected: her family's wealth was not a reward for virtue. Their influence was not a sign of divine favor. The world she had been raised to revere was built on illusion, and she could no longer pretend otherwise.

Maya had given her no answers, only more questions, but that was the gift of their friendship. It was easy to believe in the righteousness of power when it went unchallenged. It was easy to be blind when no one forced you to see.

But now Silvia saw. And she could never unsee it.

Silvia Leave Privilege

Silvia had always been aware, on some level, that her life was a performance, a carefully choreographed illusion of benevolence and virtue that masked the unyielding machinery of privilege beneath. From the moment she could speak, she had been trained in the language of her family's influence, taught to smile in a way that appeared both warm and authoritative, to tilt her chin just so when cameras flashed, to wield words like instruments of control rather than expressions of truth. And yet, it was not until that night, standing at the podium beneath the glistening chandeliers, that she understood just how deeply she had been complicit in the deception.

The charity gala was an event designed to showcase magnanimity, the annual offering of her family's wealth in service of appearances. The ballroom was filled with men and women swathed in silks and pearls, their laughter light and untroubled as they sipped wine priced beyond the earnings of the very people for whom they claimed to advocate. The cause that year was hunger relief, and the irony was lost on no one but themselves.

Silvia stood behind the podium, staring at the carefully printed words in front of her. Her father had written the speech with the same fluency he used when drafting policies that siphoned wealth upward, policies that, when questioned, were defended with rhetoric about opportunity and personal responsibility. She had read the words before, practiced them in front of her mother until her intonation was just right, but now they turned to dust in her mouth.

She looked out into the sea of gleaming faces, men and women nodding in solemn appreciation of her words, and was overcome by a terrible nausea. How many times had she watched these people pledge their support for the downtrodden while ensuring that those same people remained forever on their knees? How many times had she heard her father invoke duty and compassion while his hands shaped laws designed to crush the very notion of equity?

The applause rose in a deafening wave, wrapping around her like a noose. She forced herself to endure it, to remain composed as the cameras captured her poised gratitude. But inside, something had ruptured.

That night, alone in the vastness of her bedroom, she stared at the reflection in her mirror. A girl in an emerald gown, coiffed and polished, a portrait of privilege, an image so far removed from truth that she felt an almost physical revulsion. The weight of it all pressed down on her, suffocating in its inevitability.

She could not do this anymore.

Silvia moved with the quiet efficiency of someone acting on sheer instinct. She packed only what was necessary, a few changes of clothes, a notebook, a handful of books she could not bear to part with. A small envelope of cash, enough to get her somewhere, though she had no idea where that would be.

Before she left, she placed a note on her bed, her handwriting steady even as her heart pounded.

I can't do this anymore. I can't be part of a system that thrives on inequality and lies. I'm sorry.

She didn't look back as she slipped through the corridors of the house, past the portraits of ancestors whose wealth had been amassed on the backs of unseen laborers. The estate was silent at that hour, its opulence unbothered by the restless conscience of one of its own. She stepped into the cool night air, inhaling deeply as though it were her first breath.

For the first time in her life, she was alone.

The city stretched before her, vast and indifferent. The streets were foreign in a way she had never noticed before, their edges rougher, their shadows deeper. It was one thing to study poverty in the abstract, to read about inequity from the comfort of a leather armchair, but another entirely to walk into its unknown corridors without the safety of wealth to shield her. She felt, for the first time, what it meant to be untethered.

She spent the first night in a cheap motel, paying in cash and avoiding the gaze of the clerk behind the desk. The room was small, the sheets thin, the air thick with the scent of old smoke, but it was hers. She sat on the bed, her bag beside her, and let herself feel the enormity of what she had done. There was no plan beyond escape, no grand blueprint for reinvention. Only the certainty that she could not go back.

The following days were a study in contrasts. She walked through streets she had only ever seen from behind tinted car windows, watched as people moved with the quiet determination of survival. She took meals at small diners where no one knew or cared who she was, where her name carried no weight. It was disorienting and intoxicating in equal measure. The anonymity, the lack of expectation, it was freedom of a kind she had never known.

Yet, the reality of what she had done settled in with every passing moment. She had no practical skills, no experience beyond the curated life she had abandoned. Money, though she had brought some, would not last forever. She had spent her life preparing to lead, but what did that mean when stripped of influence? When the weight of a name meant nothing in the spaces where real lives unfolded?

Still, there was no regret. Uncertainty, yes. Fear, undeniably. But never regret. She had stepped beyond the walls that had confined her, into a world she did not yet understand but was determined to navigate. She had chosen to relinquish power rather than wield it at the expense of others, and in that choice, there was an exhilarating kind of terror.

She thought often of Maya in those early days, of the conversations they had shared in hushed tones, of the questions that had brought her to this moment. She had always known that leaving would come at a cost. Her father would see it as betrayal, her mother as a tragedy. They would search for her, not out of love but out of the need to control. But she would not be found.

Silvia had spent her life rehearsing speeches that were never her own, shaping herself into the image of what was expected. But now, stripped of all that had once defined her, she was faced with a different kind of challenge.

Who was she beyond the name she had left behind?

The answer was not yet clear. But for the first time, she was willing to search for it on her own terms.

The night air was crisp, filled with the hum of a city that never truly slept, but to Silvia, it was as if the world had momentarily paused to mark the gravity of her departure. The mansion she had called home loomed behind her, its windows glowing faintly against the dark, a symbol of all she had left behind, privilege, expectation, certainty. The great house, with its towering columns and well-manicured grounds, was an emblem of permanence, but Silvia had come to understand that its grandeur masked something brittle, something fragile that could not withstand the force of truth.

The streets stretched before her in uncertain promise. The cobbled roads, once glimpsed only through the tinted glass of chauffeured cars, now met the soles of her own feet, offering no assurances, only possibility. This was the moment she had imagined in the restless hours of night, when dreams of escape tangled with fear of the unknown. And yet, standing here, inhaling the scent of damp stone and distant kitchens closing for the evening, she found herself filled not with trepidation, but with resolve.

She had no real plan, no final destination mapped in her mind. What she carried was the certainty that she could not return, that the life her parents had so carefully constructed for her was not one she could inhabit any longer. That life had been a series of rehearsals, an endless performance of grace and intellect, a rigid adherence to scripts written long before she had drawn her first breath. And though she had played the part well, she had come to see it for what it was, a role that diminished her, that reduced her to an instrument in a great machine built to preserve power, not to dispense justice.

Silvia closed her eyes for a moment, listening to the steady rhythm of her own breathing. The weight of her decision pressed down upon her, but it was not a burden; it was an affirmation. She was leaving behind not only the walls of her father's house, but the illusions that had imprisoned her within them. And so, she did the only thing that could be done, she moved forward.

Each step felt both momentous and inconsequential, a single footfall in a world that would not pause to mark her absence. But she did not need the world's recognition; she needed only to keep walking. She carried little, some clothes, a few books, enough money to sustain her for a while, but she had something far more valuable: a mind that had been sharpened by doubt and honed by truth. Her father had taught her to think, though he had not intended for her thoughts to lead her away from him. Her mother had taught her discipline, though she had not foreseen it manifesting in such rebellion.

She reached the edge of the city, where the manicured streets gave way to uneven pavement, where the lanterns grew sparse and the sky stretched wider. Here, the air felt different, unburdened by the weight of expectation. She paused, turning once to look back at the house that had shaped her, that had sought to define her. The life she had known was behind her now, distant and untouchable, belonging to someone else.

For the first time, Silvia acknowledged what she had suspected for years, she was alone. Not in the tragic sense her mother might have imagined, but in a way that felt new and exhilarating. Her decisions were her own now, her failures and triumphs no longer dictated by the carefully managed expectations of others. The world was vast, indifferent, and utterly uncharted before her.

She whispered a prayer then, not to the God of her father's sermons, the one who had been invoked to justify wealth and dominion, but to the God she wished existed, the one who saw the worth of a soul not in its lineage but in its integrity. "Guide me," she said, her voice steady despite the whirlwind within her. "Show me the way."

And with that, she turned from the house and its memories, from the weight of a name that had once bound her, and walked toward the unknown. The path ahead was dark, uncertain, but she did not hesitate. There was no turning back, only forward, into a future that was, at last, truly hers to claim.

Chapter 2

Silvia's Departure

Silvia's departure from her family's estate was not just a physical act but a declaration of independence. She left behind the gilded cage of her upbringing, trading the opulence of her parents' mansion for the uncertainty of the unknown. The severance was absolute, her father's fury as theatrical as it was final. He declared her dead to the family, a traitor to their legacy, as if her rejection of wealth and power were not a personal conviction but an unforgivable heresy. Her mother, though less prone to dramatics, lamented not her daughter's absence but the disgrace of it. The newspapers would whisper, the invitations would thin, the family name would be spoken with a tinge of scandal. But Silvia no longer cared for the expectations that had weighed upon her shoulders since birth. For the first time in her life, she felt unshackled. She had no plan, no destination, only a burning desire to find something real, something true.

The university was a world apart from the cloistered luxury of her childhood. It was not a finishing school for the elite, where names carried weight and futures were predetermined, but a place teeming with movement and thought. She had arrived with little more than a suitcase of books and a scholarship, one granted not because of her name but in spite of it. If her father's wealth had once opened doors, her defiance had ensured that those doors would now remain firmly shut.

Silvia was unmoored but exhilarated. She had been raised in a fortress of certainty, where doctrine had been fed to her with the same assurance as bread and wine at the dinner table. But here, questions were not only permitted; they were expected. She was surrounded by students who spoke with urgency about justice, about history, about the mechanisms of power that her family had long upheld. She sat in lecture halls where professors dismantled the myths of meritocracy and traced the lineage of oppression not as an abstraction but as a living force.

At first, she merely listened, absorbing everything like dry earth after a drought. But soon, the need to do more than listen took root. It was not enough to unlearn the narratives of her childhood, she wanted to challenge them. She sought out the thinkers who did not merely analyze the world but sought to change it. She attended seminars on philosophy and political theory, debates that stretched late into the night, student gatherings where anger simmered just beneath the surface. And in these spaces, she encountered minds as restless as her own.

One of the first figures to leave an indelible mark upon her was Dr. Helen Arendt, a professor whose lectures did not simply inform but unsettle. She spoke with a conviction that left no room for pretense, dissecting the structures of capitalism and patriarchy with the precision of a surgeon. "Power," she said in one of her earliest lectures, "does not maintain itself through brute force alone. It survives because we are taught to accept it as inevitable, as natural. Your task is not merely to resist, but to redefine what is possible."

Silvia sought her out after class, eager to understand more. Dr. Arendt, ever skeptical of privileged young idealists, regarded her with measured patience. "What are you willing to risk?" she asked Silvia one evening, after a discussion on labor movements. "It is easy to renounce wealth when you still have the safety net of name and influence. What will you do when that net is truly gone?"

Silvia had no answer then. But the question haunted her.

She immersed herself in the world of activism, at first cautiously, then with fervor. She attended protests, joined reading groups, wrote articles for underground student publications. She spent nights in crowded apartments where revolutionary theories were debated over cheap wine, where plans were drawn for sit-ins and strikes. She met organizers who had spent years fighting for workers' rights, for racial justice, for an end to the very systems her family had profited from. And yet, for all the conviction that surrounded her, she began to see fissures within the movements as well.

There was ego here, too, disguised beneath rhetoric. There were those who spoke of dismantling power yet hoarded influence themselves. Silvia saw how some used activism as a stage, as a means of personal elevation rather than collective liberation. She watched as factions formed, as arguments over purity and principle led to fractures rather than unity. The disillusionment crept in, slow and insidious. Was she merely replacing one hierarchy with another?

Maya, her oldest friend and the one constant in her shifting world, listened to her doubts without judgment. "It's messy," she admitted one evening, after Silvia had vented her frustrations. "People are flawed. Even the ones fighting for justice. But that doesn't mean the fight isn't worth it."

Silvia wanted to believe her. She wanted to believe that the imperfections of the movement did not make its aims any less urgent. And so, she stayed. She continued to learn, to push, to question. She no longer sought a singular truth but understood that truth itself was fluid, that it lived in the struggle, in the refusal to accept the world as it was.

And yet, there were moments of exhaustion, when the weight of it all felt unbearable. She thought of the certainty her father wielded, the unshakeable belief in his own rightness. It had been a terrible kind of power, but it had also been simple. To question, to wrestle with complexity, to exist in the space of doubt, this was infinitely harder.

One evening, as she sat alone in the university library, surrounded by books that offered no clear answers, Dr. Arendt's question returned to her: What are you willing to risk?

Silvia closed her eyes, inhaling deeply. She had already risked her family, her name, her place in the world she had once belonged to. But was she ready to risk the new world she had entered? To not only critique but to act, even when action meant uncertainty, even when it meant failure?

She did not yet know. But she was willing to find out.

Academic Immersion & Activism

Silvia found refuge in the university, a place where ideas were currency and questions were encouraged. It was a world in motion, shifting beneath her feet with an energy that both exhilarated and unnerved her. The campus was sprawling, its buildings worn with the weight of generations of students who had passed through its halls, leaving behind echoes of their struggles and triumphs. Here, she was no longer the daughter of privilege, no longer bound by the suffocating expectations of her lineage. She was simply Silvia, a student among students, a mind among minds, a seeker in search of truth.

She had earned her place, though she knew the weight of her surname still carried whispers among those who recognized it. Her scholarship had not been bestowed out of charity or familial influence but won through sheer determination. The administration might have known her name, but her professors knew her mind, and that, at least, belonged to her alone.

At first, she was overwhelmed. The university was a world away from the sterile halls of her family's estate, teeming with life and energy, with contradictions and collisions of thought.

Students debated fiercely in the quad, their voices sharp with conviction, their gestures wild with urgency. Professors did not merely lecture but dismantled, challenged, provoked. Here, history was not a tapestry of inevitable progress but a battlefield where the victors had inscribed their version of truth. Silvia sat in lecture halls where the foundations of power were stripped bare, where the very institutions that had shaped her family's wealth and influence were examined with unsparing scrutiny.

She listened. She absorbed. She unlearned.

She had spent her life in a bubble, shielded from the struggles of the world, her understanding of hardship filtered through the detached language of policy and philanthropy. But now, she was surrounded by people who had fought for every opportunity, who carried the weight of systemic oppression on their shoulders. She sat beside students whose lives had been shaped by forces she had never truly considered, workers who studied by night and labored by day, immigrants who had crossed borders at great personal cost, activists who bore the scars of protests that had turned violent. She heard their stories, their anger, their hope, and she began to see the world through their eyes.

Maya had been right, change was not a theory to be dissected in books, nor was it merely a question of will. It was a fight, waged in the streets, in classrooms, in courtrooms, in whispered conversations behind closed doors. It was a battle against forces so entrenched that they were mistaken for the natural order of things.

Silvia's education did not remain confined to the lecture halls. She found herself drawn into the circles of student activists, into late-night gatherings where the air was thick with cigarette smoke and the fervor of revolution. There were those who spoke of justice with fire in their eyes, who argued over tactics, who believed, with unshakable conviction, that change was not only necessary but imminent. Silvia listened, captivated, but also cautious. She had been raised in a world where power was wielded with quiet calculation, where words were tools of persuasion rather than weapons of defiance. Here, power was confronted head-on, challenged, dismantled. The language was different, the energy raw.

She met people who reshaped her understanding of opposition. There was Nora, a law student who had grown up in a neighborhood where police sirens were a constant refrain, who could recite legal statutes like poetry and spoke with the sharp precision of someone who had spent a lifetime being dismissed. There was Malik, a history major whose family had been displaced by gentrification, who carried the weight of generations in his voice and saw the fight for justice as both personal and collective. There was Samira, an environmental activist who viewed capitalism and climate destruction as inseparable, who could break down economic theories as easily as she could organize a protest.

Through them, Silvia saw the complexity of oppression, not as a singular force, but as an intricate web, ensnaring people in different ways, through race, through class, through gender, through borders. And she saw, too, the flaws within the movements she admired. Activists who claimed to reject hierarchy but built their own. Leaders who demanded purity of thought, who turned on their own at the slightest deviation. Movements fractured by ego, by exhaustion, by the sheer difficulty of sustaining opposition against forces that seemed immovable.

She found herself both enthralled and disillusioned. There was something intoxicating about the certainty of those around her, about the way they threw themselves into their causes with unwavering belief. But Silvia had spent too long in the company of those who wielded power to not recognize its presence, even among those who claimed to reject it. There were those who sought control in new ways, those who relished their authority over the movement, those who turned activism into performance rather than practice.

She spoke to Maya about it one evening, their conversation stretching into the small hours of the morning.

"You see the problems," Maya said, her voice steady. "Good. That means you're thinking. But tell me, do you believe in the fight, despite the flaws?"

Silvia hesitated. "I don't know yet. I want to. But I've seen how power works. Even here."

Maya nodded. "And you will keep seeing it. But that doesn't mean you walk away. It means you fight smarter. It means you remember that the goal isn't purity, it's justice. And justice is messy."

Silvia carried those words with her in the months that followed. She threw herself deeper into the work, not seeking purity, but understanding. She attended organizing meetings, worked on mutual aid projects, helped craft policy proposals that could be taken beyond the university walls. She wrote, not for the validation of her professors, but for underground publications that spoke to the urgency of the present.

But she did not let herself be swallowed whole. She maintained a watchful distance, wary of the traps that movements could fall into. She questioned. She challenged. And sometimes, she stepped away, needing space to think, to breathe, to remind herself why she had chosen this path.

There were moments of despair, moments when she wondered if anything they did could truly shift the weight of history. She had grown up in the presence of men who shaped laws, who commanded industries, who moved the world with a flick of a pen. What did student protests mean in comparison? What did an article in a radical journal accomplish when wealth could silence dissent with a single well-placed donation?

But then, there were moments of clarity, when she saw a policy shift because of pressure from the students, when she watched a fellow organizer stand up to an administrator and win, when she heard from someone whose life had been changed by the very work she sometimes doubted. Those moments were enough to keep going.

Silvia's immersion in academia and activism was not a linear journey. It was filled with contradictions, with doubts, with missteps. But she had left behind a world where certainty had been handed to her, where the rightness of her place had been unchallenged. She had chosen a world of struggle, of complexity, of endless questioning.

And for the first time, she did not long for easy answers. She had found something far more valuable: the determination to ask better questions.

Alternative Philosophies and Political Theories

Silvia's classes became her sanctuary. She devoured books on Marxism, anarchism, and feminist theory, her mind racing with new ideas. The pages of her readings were not just words but revelations, dismantling the carefully constructed world she had once believed immutable. She found herself grappling with concepts that had been foreign to her upbringing, historical materialism, the illusion of meritocracy, the gendered divisions of labor. The professors who once seemed distant figures became guides through the labyrinth of critical thought.

One in particular stood out, Dr. Helen Arendt. A formidable presence in both the classroom and the activist community, Dr. Arendt was a scholar of both theory and action. Her lectures were not mere academic exercises but impassioned dissections of contemporary power structures. She had a way of speaking that made injustice tangible, not a thing of abstract history but a living force shaping every breath they took.

"Power," Dr. Arendt said during one lecture, "is not just about wealth or politics. It's about control, over resources, over bodies, over minds. To challenge power, you must first understand it."

Silvia took these words to heart. She was no longer satisfied with merely reading about change; she wanted to be part of it. She joined study groups where students debated strategies for dismantling oppressive systems. She attended protests that transformed theory into action, standing shoulder to shoulder with those who had been born into struggles she had only recently come to recognize. She immersed herself in the world of activism, not merely as an observer, but as a participant.

It was through these movements that Silvia met people who had dedicated their lives to fighting for justice. There was Khalid, a labor organizer who had spent years rallying workers against corporate exploitation, his voice a weapon honed through years of defiance. There was Aisha, a community advocate who worked with displaced families, whose understanding of economic disparity was drawn from lived experience rather than textbooks. Their passion, their determination, both humbled and inspired her. They were not theorists in ivory towers but individuals who bore the cost of injustice and still found the strength to resist.

As her knowledge deepened, so did her disillusionment with the world she had left behind. She thought back to the opulence of her childhood, to the quiet assurances of power that had surrounded her like an invisible cocoon. It was not just the excess that repelled her now, but the ways in which it had been justified. The rhetoric of charity and good governance had masked systemic exploitation; wealth had been framed as an indicator of virtue rather than a product of inequity. She could no longer look at her past without seeing its complicity in the suffering of others.

Yet Silvia was also learning that radical thought was not free from contradiction. Within these movements she admired, there were fractures, clashes of ideology, strategic disagreements, power struggles that mirrored the very systems they sought to dismantle. She watched as organizations splintered over questions of purity versus pragmatism. She saw leaders denounce hierarchy while unconsciously replicating it.

She wrestled with these tensions. It was easier to believe in a clear enemy, in a monolithic force of oppression that could be toppled through sheer will. But the truth was more complicated. Systems were not upheld by villains alone but by people, ordinary, fearful, self-interested. And even among those who resisted, the weight of history and ego often created new barriers to collective liberation.

She spoke to Dr. Arendt about these doubts one evening, seeking clarity.

"Movements are flawed," Dr. Arendt admitted, "because people are flawed. But that does not negate the fight. It means you engage critically. You work for change not because the struggle is pure, but because the alternative is complacency."

Silvia carried those words with her. She did not seek perfection, but progress. She continued her studies, not as an escape from action, but as a means to strengthen it. She honed her writing, using her words to dismantle the narratives that upheld the status quo. She learned to navigate the delicate balance between hope and realism, between idealism and the harsh pragmatism that true change required.

And through it all, she never stopped questioning. She understood now that there was no single path to justice, no universal formula for liberation. There was only the work, the constant, relentless work of reimagining and rebuilding, of opposing and reshaping. And she was ready to devote herself to it.

Progress is Persistence

As Silvia delved deeper into academia and activism, she began to notice the cracks in these worlds as well. The idealism she had admired from a distance was often overshadowed by ego and infighting. The same sharp rhetoric that once inspired her now revealed a different truth: not all who spoke of justice truly sought it. Some were drawn more to the performance of activism than to its practice, their commitment to change often as fleeting as the news cycle that dictated their relevance.

Activists competed for recognition, their causes reduced to hashtags and soundbites, their battles waged as much for visibility as for victory. Academics, too, were not exempt from this performance. Silvia watched as complex theories were hoarded within ivory towers, published in papers dense with jargon, their insights rendered inaccessible to those who needed them most. The words that should have been weapons against oppression were instead locked behind paywalls, turned into intellectual currency rather than tools for liberation.

One incident stood out in particular. Silvia had attended a rally for climate justice, her heart swelling with hope as she listened to the speakers, their voices rising above the crowd with passion and urgency. For a moment, she believed she had found something untainted, something real. But afterward, as the crowds thinned and the energy faded, she overheard two organizers arguing over who deserved credit for the event's success. Their words were sharp, their tone bitter, and Silvia felt a pang of disappointment. The movement had seemed so unified, so resolute, until she glimpsed the rivalries beneath the surface.

"Is this what it's all about?" she asked Maya during one of their late-night calls. "Fighting for the spotlight instead of fighting for change?"

Maya sighed. "It's complicated, Silvia. People are flawed. Movements are flawed. But that doesn't mean they're not worth fighting for."

Silvia wanted to believe her. She wanted to believe that the fight was still worth it, that justice could be pursued even amidst imperfection. But the doubt lingered. She had left her family's world of performative piety only to find performative morality in its place. The same contradictions she had fled seemed to follow her, cloaked in different language, framed in different ideologies but no less present.

The people who claimed to despise power still sought it, only in different forms. Those who spoke of inclusivity wielded exclusion as a weapon. The very systems they condemned, hierarchy, dominance, control, replicated themselves in their own ranks. And so Silvia found herself in yet another world where authenticity was secondary to appearance, where the righteousness of a cause did not always guarantee the integrity of those who championed it.

Her disappointment deepened as she encountered more instances of hypocrisy, both in academia and activism. She watched as professors who lectured on justice exploited their graduate students for unpaid labor. She saw activists shame others for failing to meet impossible standards of ideological purity while refusing to acknowledge their own blind spots. The institutions she had believed in, even those built around radical critique, seemed unable to escape the very forces they opposed.

In the classroom, Silvia found herself increasingly frustrated by the widening gap between theory and action. She sat through discussions on economic justice, yet the students who spoke most passionately about wealth redistribution came from families who had never known financial insecurity. She attended seminars on systemic racism, yet noticed how few students of color had the privilege of sitting in those rooms. When she raised these contradictions, she was often met with deflection, as if acknowledging these failings would undermine the validity of their work. But to Silvia, refusing to confront these hypocrisies made the work hollow.

She turned her attention to the activist spaces she had once found so energizing, only to find similar disillusionment. She joined a direct-action group focused on tenants' rights, eager to engage in meaningful, tangible work. At first, she was invigorated by the efforts, organizing rent strikes, meeting with struggling families, disrupting predatory landlords. But soon, she began to notice the same dynamics she had seen elsewhere. Certain organizers took center stage while others were relegated to the margins. Internal power struggles dominated meetings, often at the expense of the very people they were meant to serve.

One evening, after a particularly contentious meeting, she found herself walking alone, replaying the arguments in her head. The discussion had been about tactics, but it had devolved into personal attacks, accusations of ideological impurity. "If you're not willing to risk arrest, are you really committed?" one organizer had demanded. "If you're not prepared to lose everything, are you really on our side?" The words had unsettled her. Silvia had given up wealth, security, family, was that not enough? And yet, she had seen the cost of absolutism before. It was a dangerous thing to demand purity over participation.

She called Maya again, desperate for reassurance. "How do you stay in it? How do you keep fighting when it feels like everyone's tearing each other apart?"

Maya was quiet for a moment. "Because the alternative is worse," she finally said. "Because the system wants us divided. Because even when movements are flawed, they're still necessary."

Silvia nodded, though she remained unconvinced. She did not want to abandon the fight. She knew too much to turn away. But she also knew she could not ignore what she had seen. The fractures were too deep, the contradictions too glaring. The path forward felt less certain than ever.

She resolved, then, to tread carefully, not in cynicism, but in awareness. She would no longer mistake rhetoric for action, nor visibility for virtue. The cause of justice was still hers, but she would not let herself be deceived by those who wore its banner for their own ends. She would remain critical, not to undermine, but to strengthen. She would seek truth, not in grand performances, but in the quiet, persistent work of real change.

And she would remember, always, that the struggle was not about perfection, but persistence. That justice was not an abstract ideal, but something to be built, brick by imperfect brick. And she would keep building, even if the walls around her threatened to crumble.

Keep Asking Questions

One evening, Silvia sat in the university library, surrounded by stacks of books and notes. The dim light from the desk lamp cast long shadows across the pages, its soft glow failing to illuminate the questions that crowded her mind. The words in front of her blurred together, tangled in thoughts too restless to be corralled by the discipline of study. She had spent months in pursuit of knowledge, and yet, at that moment, she felt no closer to certainty than when she had first arrived.

She leaned back in her chair, rubbing her temples. The weight of her disillusionment pressed down upon her. She had come here searching for truth, for understanding, for something to hold onto in a world that seemed more contradictory the deeper she examined it. But all she had found were layers upon layers of complexity, endless contradictions, endless questions with no simple answers.

"What am I even doing here?" she whispered to herself, her voice barely audible over the rustling pages of other students buried in their own pursuits.

A voice interrupted her thoughts. "Looking for answers, I assume."

Silvia looked up to see Dr. Arendt standing nearby, arms crossed, a knowing smile playing at her lips. There was something steady about her presence, something that made Silvia feel both seen and challenged.

Silvia sighed, closing the book in front of her. "I don't know if I'll ever find them."

Dr. Arendt moved to the chair across from her and sat down, the edges of her worn leather bag brushing against the table. "Maybe not," she said, "but the search is what matters. Keep asking questions. Keep challenging the status quo. That's how change happens."

Silvia considered this, her gaze drifting to the open book in front of her. The search. It had become a relentless force in her life, driving her forward, compelling her to dismantle and rebuild everything she had once believed in. But was that enough? Was it possible to live in constant interrogation, to exist in a state of perpetual questioning without ever arriving at an answer?

Dr. Arendt seemed to read the doubt on her face. "You're looking for certainty, Silvia. But certainty is a trap. People cling to it because it's comfortable, because it gives them a sense of control. But the truth, the real truth, is never that simple."

Silvia exhaled slowly. She had spent her childhood in a world of absolutes, where wealth was deserved, power was ordained, and questioning was rebellion. Now, she lived in a world where certainty itself felt like an illusion. It was an exhausting way to exist, but it was also the only way she could.

"I used to think I would get to a point where everything would make sense," Silvia admitted. "That if I learned enough, if I fought hard enough, I would reach some kind of clarity."

Dr. Arendt smiled, shaking her head. "If clarity were the goal, none of us would be here. The best minds in history weren't the ones who found answers. They were the ones who refused to stop asking questions."

Silvia let the words settle. The exhaustion in her bones did not dissipate, but her resolve hardened. She didn't have all the answers. She might never have them. But she could not go back, not to the empty certainty of her past, not to the illusions of her upbringing. The only way forward was through the uncertainty, through the doubt, through the relentless search for something more.

She looked back at Dr. Arendt. "So I just… keep searching?"

Dr. Arendt nodded. "You keep searching. You keep learning. And when you see injustice, you fight it. Not because you know exactly how to fix everything, but because doing nothing is not an option."

Silvia nodded, her fingers tightening around the edge of the book in front of her. The questions would never end. The contradictions would never fully resolve. But she would not let that stop her. She had chosen this path, and she would walk it, step by uncertain step.

Dr. Arendt stood, adjusting the strap of her bag. "Get some rest, Silvia. The revolution will still be here in the morning."

Silvia allowed herself a small smile as she watched her professor disappear into the dimly lit rows of bookshelves. Then, with a steadying breath, she turned back to her notes and picked up her pen. The search continued.

But as she sat there, pen poised above her notebook, she found herself lingering on Dr. Arendt's words. Keep searching. Keep fighting. It was a mantra she had heard before, but it felt different now. The weight of it was heavier, more real. It was not simply an intellectual exercise; it was a commitment, a way of being in the world.

Her thoughts drifted to the movements she had been part of, the people she had met. She thought of Maya, who still believed despite all the fractures. She thought of Khalid, who had been organizing workers long before she had even learned the word exploitation. She thought of the tenants she had helped defend, the students who had shared their stories with her, the activists who had given everything for a world they might never live to see. They were not perfect, but they were persistent. And that persistence mattered.

Silvia closed her notebook and leaned back in her chair, staring at the ceiling. She realized then that she had been thinking about it all wrong. She had been searching for an endpoint, for a moment where everything would click into place and she would understand exactly what to do. But that moment would never come. There would always be doubt, always be struggle. The work would never be finished. And maybe that was the point.

She turned back to her book, but this time, she read with a different intention. She was not searching for answers. She was learning how to live within the questions. She was preparing herself, not for certainty, but for the endless, necessary, beautiful fight ahead.

Chapter 3

A Growing Realization

Silvia's initial excitement about academia and activism began to wane as she delved deeper into these worlds. What had once seemed like a sanctuary of ideas and ideals now felt like a battleground of egos and agendas. The spaces that promised intellectual rigor and moral conviction often proved themselves to be arenas of self-interest, where visibility mattered more than truth, and where the pursuit of justice often masked a more human, more personal hunger for validation.

Silvia observed the strange paradox of scholars who built their reputations on critiquing power, only to wield it in ways eerily reminiscent of those they opposed. She sat through lectures where professors spoke grandly of the dangers of capitalism while privately lobbying for corporate-backed research funding. Some academics presented themselves as champions of the marginalized, yet they operated in institutions that perpetuated the very hierarchies they denounced. Their words, lofty and carefully measured, often seemed detached from the realities they claimed to analyze.

Within activist circles, Silvia was similarly unsettled by the contradictions she encountered. Many who claimed to reject authority replicated the same structures of exclusion and control within their own movements. Those who spoke of collectivism and shared struggle often expected unwavering loyalty to their personal leadership. Even in radical spaces, where hierarchy was meant to be abolished, it persisted in subtle but insidious forms, who was invited to speak at conferences, who controlled access to resources, who dictated the rhetoric and tactics of the movement.

One particular meeting cemented Silvia's unease. She had been attending strategy sessions for a local labor solidarity network, a group ostensibly dedicated to building power for workers. Yet, during one gathering, the conversation veered sharply away from the pressing concerns of the workers themselves and into a dispute between two senior organizers over who had been more instrumental in securing recent policy changes. The discussion turned into a tense battle of egos, with each person eager to cement their legacy rather than focus on the work at hand.

Silvia found herself caught between admiration and skepticism. She had met individuals within these spaces who were deeply committed, who sacrificed comfort and security to fight for what they believed in. But for every genuine advocate, there seemed to be another who was using activism as a ladder, whether to social prestige, professional advancement, or ideological dominance over others.

She confided in Maya one evening, her frustration bubbling over. "Why does it always turn into this? Why does every movement, every intellectual space, seem to collapse under its own weight?"

Maya, who had been involved in radical politics for years, smiled ruefully. "Because people bring their flaws with them, no matter what the cause is. Power doesn't just go away, it changes form. Even in spaces that are supposed to be different, the same struggles over control, recognition, and influence emerge."

Silvia absorbed this in silence. She had assumed that leaving the world of wealth and influence would mean escaping these dynamics, but the reality was more complicated. Power was not confined to institutions or political parties; it existed wherever people gathered, even those who had sworn to oppose it.

She became wary of the symbols of credibility that governed these worlds, the carefully curated language of academia, the social capital of being recognized as a leading activist, the unspoken hierarchy of whose voices carried the most weight. She noticed how critiques of oppression were sometimes wielded less as tools for justice and more as weapons to discredit opponents. She saw how accusations of ideological impurity could be used to silence dissent rather than encourage growth.

The longer she stayed, the more she recognized the emotional cost of existing in these spaces. The relentless cycles of internal conflict, the need to constantly prove one's commitment, the way success was often measured not in material improvements but in social capital. It was exhausting. And yet, she could not bring herself to walk away completely.

The alternative, the complacency she had rejected in her old life, was unthinkable. Silvia still believed in the need for change, even if she now doubted the purity of the structures meant to achieve it. But she realized that her relationship to activism and intellectual inquiry had to change. She could no longer afford to believe in spaces as inherently good or inherently bad; she had to navigate them with awareness, understanding that every movement, every institution, was shaped by the human impulses that created them.

In time, she adjusted her expectations. She stopped expecting perfection from intellectual circles, understanding that they, too, were shaped by institutional pressures. She became more discerning about the activists she aligned herself with, searching not for those who performed their beliefs most eloquently but those who worked, quietly and consistently, toward real solutions. She learned to recognize when a debate was more about ego than about justice, when a critique was meant to build and when it was meant to destroy.

Most importantly, she learned to trust her own instincts. She had spent so much of her life looking for a framework, a system, a movement that would offer her certainty. But certainty, she now understood, was the most dangerous illusion of all. She was willing to live with doubt, willing to fight even without perfect clarity. What mattered was not the purity of any ideology but the tangible impact of her choices. She could not fix the flaws of every institution or prevent every act of hypocrisy, but she could choose, moment by moment, to act with integrity herself.

And that, she decided, would have to be enough.

Expectations

Determined to find a system of thought that aligned with her values, Silvia began to explore different ideologies. She immersed herself in political discourse, reading manifestos, attending debates, and seeking out those who had dedicated their lives to the pursuit of justice. She sat in dimly lit university halls, absorbing lectures on Marxism, anarchism, and eco-socialism, each promising a path to a more just and equitable world. And yet, the more she learned, the more disillusioned she became.

Marxism, with its emphasis on class struggle and historical materialism, resonated with her on an intellectual level. It provided a coherent critique of capitalism, exposing the ways in which economic systems oppressed the working class. Yet, as she examined its applications, she found herself troubled by its rigidity. The theory, while powerful, often failed to account for the nuances of identity, culture, and the deeply personal dimensions of oppression. In many circles, adherence to Marxist thought was expected to be unwavering, and deviations from doctrine were met with suspicion. Silvia found it difficult to reconcile this dogmatic rigidity with the complexity of human experience. She had witnessed inequality not just through class, but through race, gender, and history, factors that were often dismissed as secondary within traditional Marxist frameworks.

Anarchism, by contrast, thrilled her. It spoke of radical freedom, of the dismantling of all unjust hierarchies, of self-governance and direct action. She admired the refusal to place faith in institutions and was drawn to its emphasis on mutual aid and community-driven solutions. Yet, she soon found herself troubled by its limitations. While the rejection of power structures made sense in theory, Silvia struggled to envision a world entirely without organization, without leadership in some form. She saw how even within anarchist collectives, authority crept back in, hidden beneath informal structures, with influence coalescing around charismatic individuals. Could there truly be a movement without hierarchy, when human nature so often seemed to recreate power in new forms?

Eco-socialism, on the other hand, offered a vision of harmony, of a society in which economic justice was entwined with environmental sustainability. It was an ideology that called for a rejection of both capitalist excess and exploitative industrial models, seeking instead a future in which humanity and nature coexisted rather than competed. But in practice, she found its proponents too often lost in abstract theorizing. Grand ideas of ecological balance and post-capitalist sustainability were discussed at length, yet the steps to make them reality felt frustratingly vague. She saw activists who spoke about sustainable futures but remained disconnected from the immediate struggles of poverty, of housing, of labor. Could one truly discuss the future without first reckoning with the dire present?

As Silvia deepened her study, she began to notice a pattern. Every ideology was, at its core, an attempt to impose order upon chaos, to offer a theory of justice that could be applied universally. And yet, each failed to fully encapsulate the messy, unpredictable reality of human life. No system was as seamless as its adherents claimed. The theorists of one school dismissed the insights of another, too preoccupied with ideological purity to see where their ideas might complement rather than compete.

She sat in on bitter debates, where radicals accused one another of betrayal for engaging in electoral politics, where idealists dismissed pragmatic concerns in favor of theoretical purity. She watched as factions split over minor doctrinal differences, their energy focused inward rather than outward toward real change. The same egos and power struggles she had observed in academia and activism seemed to manifest even in these supposedly revolutionary spaces. Was this the inevitable fate of all human efforts? To replicate, in some new form, the very power structures they sought to dismantle?

Silvia found herself retreating, watching rather than participating, questioning rather than accepting. She did not want to be trapped in endless critique, but she also refused to accept any framework uncritically. She longed for a synthesis, for something that acknowledged the structural injustices Marxists exposed, the radical freedom anarchists envisioned, and the ecological balance eco-socialists demanded, without requiring her to adhere to any one school of thought completely. But the more she sought such a path, the more elusive it became.

One evening, as she sat in the library, surrounded by books that promised different answers yet all seemed to leave something out, she felt an overwhelming sense of exhaustion. She had left behind the certainties of her upbringing, the comfortable lies that had been told to her about wealth and power. She had hoped to replace them with truth, with a new certainty rooted in justice. But certainty, she now realized, was a thing she might never find. And perhaps, she thought, that was not a failure but a lesson in itself.

She met with Dr. Arendt the next day, seeking guidance. "What if there isn't one right system?" she asked. "What if every ideology is just another imperfect attempt to explain something too big to be contained in a single theory?"

Dr. Arendt smiled, as though she had been waiting for Silvia to ask this. "Then perhaps the goal isn't to find the perfect system, but to keep questioning, keep learning. Theory is useful, but it is not absolute. The world will always be more complex than our best ideas about it."

Silvia considered this. She did not feel relief, exactly. She still longed for something more concrete, something that could anchor her in the chaos. But she also felt a shift within herself. She had been searching for the ideology that would provide all the answers, but maybe the real work was in embracing the contradictions, in understanding that justice was not something that could be captured in a single framework, but something that had to be built, day by day, in the choices she made.

She left the meeting feeling different, not certain, not at peace, but perhaps, for the first time, willing to sit with the uncertainty. The search was not over, but it no longer felt like a desperate attempt to find something infallible. It felt, instead, like the beginning of something more honest.

Just Show Up

The breaking point came during a heated debate in one of her classes. The topic was the role of the state in achieving social justice, and the discussion quickly devolved into a shouting match. Silvia listened as her classmates argued over abstract concepts, their words filled with passion but devoid of empathy. She watched as one student fervently defended government intervention, citing historical precedents and economic models, while another dismissed the state entirely, insisting that all structures of power were inherently oppressive.

As the voices grew louder, the arguments less about justice and more about intellectual superiority, Silvia felt a familiar sense of unease settle over her. This was not the search for truth she had envisioned, it was a performance, a contest of rhetoric, a battle for ideological dominance where real human suffering was reduced to theoretical debate.

"You're all missing the point," she finally interjected, her voice trembling with frustration. "It's not about which ideology is right or wrong. It's about the people who are suffering while we sit here debating semantics."

The room fell silent, and Silvia felt a surge of anger and despair. She had come to academia and activism seeking truth and justice, but all she had found were more lies and contradictions. She had once believed that intellectual spaces would provide answers, but now she saw how often they functioned as places of posturing rather than real engagement with the world's injustices.

Later that evening, she found herself walking aimlessly through the city, the sounds of traffic and distant conversations mingling in the cold air. She thought about the factory workers she had met at an organizing meeting, about the single mother she had spoken to at a housing rally, about the immigrant families fighting to stay in their homes. None of them had the luxury of debating policy in a classroom. They were too busy surviving, too busy struggling against the very systems being dissected in abstract terms by those who would never feel their consequences.

It was a realization that unsettled her to the core. All systems were flawed, not just in their execution, but in their very conception. Capitalism, socialism, anarchism, each claimed to be the answer, yet none could fully account for the complexity of human suffering. Each built its theory upon a vision of the world that was, at best, incomplete.

She spent the next few weeks grappling with this truth, trying to make sense of what it meant for her own beliefs. She still wanted to fight for justice, but how? How could she commit herself to any ideology when every one of them fell short? How could she continue her studies when she no longer believed in the framework that shaped them?

One evening, she met with Dr. Arendt, disheartened and frustrated. "I don't know what I believe anymore," Silvia admitted, her voice weary. "Every system, every movement, every solution feels like another layer of control, another way to justify power. How do you choose a path forward when all the paths are flawed?"

Dr. Arendt studied her for a moment before responding. "You stop looking for perfection," she said. "You stop searching for a system that has all the answers, because it doesn't exist. The work isn't about choosing the right ideology. It's about showing up. It's about doing what you can, where you can, even when it feels inadequate."

Silvia let the words sink in. She had been searching for certainty, for a framework that could hold all of her convictions without contradiction. But perhaps certainty itself was the problem. Perhaps the pursuit of ideological purity was nothing more than another form of complacency, an excuse to stand still rather than move forward.

She thought about the factory workers, the tenants, the organizers she had met. They did not wait for perfection. They fought in imperfect ways, within imperfect systems, because the alternative was silence. And maybe that was enough. Maybe that was all anyone could do.

That night, Silvia did not feel at peace, but she felt something new, acceptance. Not of injustice, not of complacency, but of the imperfection of the struggle itself. The world would always be flawed. Movements would always be messy. But the fight for justice was not about purity; it was about persistence.

And so, she resolved to persist.

Moment of Clarity

That night, Silvia sat alone in her dorm room, surrounded by books and notes. The desk lamp cast a dim glow, illuminating the disorder of her research, pages covered in annotations, half-read books stacked precariously, notebooks filled with hastily scribbled questions that seemed to multiply rather than resolve. She felt exhausted, not just physically but emotionally and spiritually. She had spent so much time searching for answers, but the more she searched, the more lost she felt.

Her professors had told her that knowledge was power, that understanding history and theory would guide her to the truth. But now, she wasn't so sure. She had studied ideologies that promised liberation, movements that had fought to reshape the world, and yet, in every one of them, she had found contradictions, blind spots, unintended consequences. There were no pure answers, only the illusions of certainty.

She ran a hand through her hair and sighed. The weight of it all pressed on her, the expectations of academia, the rhetoric of activism, the pressure to find a position, a stance, an unshakable belief. But she no longer wanted certainty. Certainty had failed her.

As she stared at the blank page of her journal, a thought occurred to her: perhaps the problem wasn't the ideologies themselves, but the way they were wielded. Perhaps the real enemy wasn't capitalism or patriarchy or the state, but the human tendency to turn ideas into dogma, to use them as tools of control rather than liberation. How many revolutions had become new tyrannies? How many truths had been twisted into instruments of exclusion?

She picked up her pen and began to write, her hand moving instinctively, as if the words had been waiting for her all along.

The truth is not in the systems we create, but in the way we live our lives. If we want to change the world, we must first change ourselves.

She paused, staring at the sentence. It wasn't an answer, but it was a start. Perhaps real change did not come from ideological purity or from finding the perfect system, but from the refusal to become complacent, from the constant interrogation of one's own actions, from the everyday choices that shaped reality more than manifestos ever could.

She closed the journal but did not move from her chair. Her mind wandered to those she had met since leaving home, the activists, the scholars, the laborers whose struggles were not theoretical but urgent, immediate. She thought of the woman who had described being priced out of her own neighborhood, the factory worker who had spent years fighting for a living wage, the undocumented student fearful of being torn from the only life they had ever known. Their problems were not abstractions. Their world did not wait for ideological perfection; it demanded action, flawed and incomplete though it might be.

Her eyes drifted back to her notes, to the dense theoretical texts she had spent months devouring. She wondered now if she had been reading them not to understand the world, but to delay having to face it. Theory had become a safe harbor, a place to shelter from the storm of reality. But justice was not built in the pages of books. It was forged in the choices people made each day, in the imperfect and often frustrating work of pushing forward despite uncertainty.

She exhaled slowly, feeling the tension in her shoulders ease just slightly. The world was vast, complicated, and often cruel, but it was also alive with possibility. She would keep questioning, keep learning, but she would also act. She would listen, not just to the voices she found in books, but to the ones speaking around her, the ones who did not need ideological perfection to know what they deserved.

She turned off the lamp and climbed into bed, allowing herself, for once, to rest. Tomorrow would bring new questions, new contradictions, but for the first time in a long while, she did not fear them. She welcomed them.

Chapter 4

Ascetic Change

Exhausted by the endless debates and disillusioned by the hypocrisy she encountered in academia and activism, Silvia made a radical decision: she would strip her life down to its bare essentials. She sold most of her possessions, donated the money to a local mutual aid fund, and moved into a small, sparsely furnished apartment on the outskirts of the city.

Her new lifestyle was a stark contrast to the opulence of her upbringing. She owned only what she needed, a few changes of clothes, a handful of books, and a laptop for her studies. She cooked simple meals, walked everywhere instead of driving, and spent her free time reading and reflecting. At first, the simplicity was liberating. She felt lighter, freer, as if she had shed not just material possessions but the weight of societal expectations.

Her new home was a stark contrast to the opulent estate of her childhood. A small, sparsely furnished apartment on the outskirts of the city, its walls bare, its rooms quiet. The silence was a companion she had not yet learned how to keep. At first, there was relief. The shedding of possessions felt like the shedding of expectation, of performance, of false security. She walked everywhere, no longer bound to the world of cars and convenience. She prepared simple meals, finding a quiet satisfaction in the rhythm of cooking, in the tangible work of caring for her own needs. She spent her days reading, reflecting, journaling, immersing herself in an existence unencumbered by excess.

And yet, solitude proved a double-edged sword. What at first felt like liberation soon became an ache of isolation. Without the noise of academia, without the urgency of activism, without the structure of a world she had rejected, she found herself adrift. The act of negation, of rejecting, stripping away, dismantling, was easy. But what was she meant to build in its place? She had escaped the performance of righteousness, but in doing so, had she made herself irrelevant to the fight she once believed in?

She missed conversation, missed the collision of ideas, missed the feeling of being a part of something larger than herself. She had left behind a world full of contradictions, but she had not yet found a space that felt whole. Doubt crept in, whispering that perhaps withdrawal was no solution, that meaning could not be found in mere rejection. She did not want to retreat from the world, she realized, she wanted to change it. And yet, how did one begin such a task when every system, every ideology, seemed flawed?

It was in the pages of an old radical zine, tucked away in the dusty back corner of a used bookstore, that she found her next step. A description of an urban commune, an intentional community built on the rejection of capitalism, a space where wealth and hierarchy were dismantled, where people lived not in competition but in cooperation. The language of the article resonated with her longing: "a new world within the shell of the old." Here was something different, not just critique, but creation.

She felt the stirrings of curiosity, of possibility. If there was a place where people truly lived according to the values she had fought for, then perhaps she had been too quick to resign herself to solitude. She had spent so much time analyzing the brokenness of the world, maybe it was time to see if another way was possible.

With a quiet determination, she packed a few things into her bag and set off toward the commune, toward the unknown, toward the possibility of rediscovering purpose in a world that had thus far failed to offer her one.

The commune was housed in what had once been a sprawling industrial warehouse, a relic of the old world's insatiable hunger for production and commerce. Its transformation was a statement in itself, walls adorned with bold murals depicting scenes of opposition, slogans scrawled in defiant brushstrokes: "Another world is possible," "Abolish wealth, embrace community," "No masters, no bosses." The air carried the scent of fresh earth from the rooftop garden, mingled with the acrid tang of paint and wood smoke from the communal kitchen. This was not merely a residence; it was a vision, a refusal to conform to the structures Silvia had spent so long resisting.

The residents of the commune were as diverse in background as they were united in purpose, activists, artists, anarchists, displaced workers, and scholars who had walked away from institutions they deemed complicit in exploitation. Their rejection of private ownership was absolute; everything was shared, from food to clothing, tools to knowledge. Each person contributed what they could, whether it was tending the gardens, cooking meals, repairing bikes, or facilitating discussions on mutual aid and collective opposition. The community thrived on the principle that no individual should hold power over another, that labor should be cooperative rather than coerced, that resources should flow according to need, not status.

Silvia, still raw from the contradictions and hierarchies she had witnessed in academia and activism, felt a deep and immediate sense of belonging. Here, the debates were not empty posturing but vital discussions with real-world applications. She joined in, eager to immerse herself in the principles that governed this space. She worked in the kitchen, kneading bread and chopping vegetables rescued from supermarket dumpsters, learning how to make do without reliance on capitalist supply chains. She attended workshops on sustainable agriculture, studied methods of direct action, and participated in heated conversations about dismantling corporate control over daily life. There was an energy here, a determination that things could be different, that change was not an abstraction but a daily practice.

The commune's commitment to self-sufficiency was impressive. They grew much of their own food in the rooftop garden, using compost from their waste and collecting rainwater for irrigation. Solar panels powered their lighting, and a makeshift wind turbine stood in the courtyard, a testament to their rejection of reliance on fossil fuels. What they could not produce themselves, they scavenged or bartered for, fostering networks of solidarity with other radical collectives throughout the city. A free store stood near the entrance, filled with clothing, books, and household goods that anyone could take as needed. Money, they insisted, had no place here.

For the first time in years, Silvia felt as though she had found what she had been searching for, not just in theory but in practice. The hypocrisy that had driven her away from her previous life seemed absent here. People did not simply talk about equality and justice; they enacted it in their daily lives. Decisions were made by consensus, and responsibilities were shared without coercion. Every morning, the residents gathered for a brief meeting to discuss the needs of the day, distributing tasks based on interest and ability rather than obligation. The structure was loose, fluid, adapting to circumstances rather than imposing rigid schedules.

She felt lighter, unburdened by the weight of expectation and contradiction that had plagued her before. She found solace in the ritual of communal meals, eating together not as an obligation but as a celebration of collective effort. Laughter rang through the vast halls in the evenings, accompanied by music from a battered old guitar or spontaneous poetry readings. It was a kind of harmony she had never experienced before, a way of living that did not feel imposed but organic, intuitive.

As she settled into the rhythm of this new life, Silvia allowed herself to believe that she had finally found a place free from the power structures she had spent so long trying to escape. She had left behind the privilege and disillusionment of her former world, stepping into something that felt authentic, tangible. Here, she told herself, was a blueprint for what society could be, if only people had the courage to reject the systems that oppressed them.

Yet beneath the surface, there were questions she had not yet dared to ask, cracks she had not yet noticed. For now, though, she let herself bask in the possibility of this world, convinced that she had finally found a space where people truly lived by their ideals, where she was no longer adrift, but part of something real.

Hidden Hierarchies

At first, Silvia believed she had found what she had long been searching for: a space where people truly lived by their values, a community untainted by the structures of power and exploitation she had fought to escape. But as the weeks passed, the illusion began to fray, the once-invisible fissures growing too apparent to ignore. What had seemed an oasis of equality and mutual care slowly revealed itself to be a microcosm of the very systems it claimed to reject.

Silvia began to notice that power, though unspoken, was concentrated in the hands of Jonah and Mara, the charismatic couple who had co-founded the commune. They spoke of consensus, of horizontal organization, yet their words carried a weight that others' did not. Decisions, though presented as collective, were often guided by their preferences, their vision shaping the trajectory of the community. When suggestions arose that contradicted their ideas, they were met with vague affirmations but seldom enacted. Those who persisted in questioning were subtly pushed aside, their voices drowned in the collective hum of agreement that had, in truth, become mere performance.

She watched as labor fell unevenly across the group. While some residents, particularly the newer arrivals, toiled tirelessly, hauling water, tending the gardens, cooking meals for dozens, others, often those closest to Jonah and Mara, seemed to float above the fray. They occupied themselves with more esoteric tasks, drafting manifestos, hosting discussion circles, theorizing about the collapse of capitalism, while the practical burdens fell upon fewer shoulders. Silvia could not help but recognize the irony: they had rejected the capitalist economy, yet here was another form of inequity, unspoken but deeply felt.

When she first raised concerns, she was met with understanding nods, with assurances that such imbalances were natural and would self-correct. But when she pressed further, the response shifted. She found herself subtly reprimanded, not through direct admonishment, but through careful reframing. Was she not being divisive? Was she not allowing doubt to cloud her belief in the project? Was she not replicating the very systems they had sought to abolish by fixating on roles and responsibilities? The weight of collective expectation pressed against her questions, urging her into silent compliance.

The language of the commune was one of liberation, but Silvia began to feel something closer to control. To challenge Jonah and Mara was to challenge the very identity of the community, and those who did so risked alienation. It was never explicit, no one was cast out, no one was scolded in the way she had seen in traditional hierarchies, but there were subtler methods of silencing. Invitations to meetings ceased. Conversations quieted when dissenters approached. Their presence became tolerated rather than welcomed.

More troubling still was the way in which the commune's values, once so compelling, began to feel less like guiding principles and more like dogma. There was little room for nuance, for questioning whether their model could be improved. The world beyond was framed in stark binaries: inside the commune was a space of freedom and authenticity; outside was the realm of corruption and false consciousness. Those who left were spoken of in muted tones, their departures rationalized as personal failures rather than systemic critiques.

Silvia's disillusionment deepened. She had once believed that by rejecting the structures of power, by living outside the boundaries of capitalism, she would find truth. But here was another system, no less flawed, no less susceptible to human frailty. The commune had its rulers, though they would never admit to the title. It had its outcasts, though it claimed radical inclusion. It had its laborers and its privileged, though it professed equality. The names of the roles had changed, but the dynamics remained the same.

One evening, as she sat in the common space watching a group argue over a resource-allocation decision that Jonah had already quietly settled, she felt a deep and weary clarity settle over her. She was witnessing a repetition of history, another failed attempt to build utopia on the shaky foundation of human imperfection. And perhaps, she thought, it was not merely the commune that had failed, but the very idea that escape was possible.

The weight of this realization pressed heavily upon her. She did not yet know what it meant for her, nor what she would do with it. But she knew one thing for certain: the certainty she had once clung to had dissolved, leaving behind only questions.

The unraveling came quietly at first, whispers caught in passing, small inconsistencies that Silvia tried to ignore. But the moment of revelation struck with the force of a tidal wave, Jonah and Mara, the supposed visionaries of this radical space, had been hoarding resources. While preaching the virtues of shared labor and mutual aid, they had quietly accumulated luxuries denied to others: high-end electronics hidden behind stacks of repurposed books, carefully portioned food reserves that never seemed to diminish for them, cash siphoned from the commune's collective contributions.

At first, Silvia refused to believe it. Surely there was an explanation. Perhaps, as they would surely argue, these things had been set aside for emergencies, for the preservation of the collective. But the deeper she dug, the more undeniable it became. The sense of betrayal hollowed her. Jonah and Mara were not simply hypocrites; they were architects of the very power imbalance they had claimed to dismantle. The ideology they had woven so tightly around the commune was, in the end, a net designed to keep others bound, while they maneuvered freely within its constraints.

The night she confronted them, the atmosphere in the commune was hushed, the air thick with unspoken understanding. Jonah, ever the charismatic orator, turned his disappointment upon her like a weapon. He did not deny her accusations. Instead, he rebranded them as symptoms of her own failure.

"Silvia," he sighed, shaking his head. "You're falling into the same trap as the world outside. You see division where there should be unity. You question leadership when what we need is trust."

Mara, standing beside him with her arms crossed, added, "Maybe this isn't the right place for you anymore. If you can't be part of the collective, maybe you're not ready for true liberation."

Silvia had no words. The walls of ideology they had built around themselves were impenetrable, their rhetoric designed to silence dissent rather than foster accountability. The very structure she had trusted to be different was, at its core, just another replication of the systems she had sought to escape.

She felt the eyes of others upon her, watching, waiting, weighing the consequences of siding with her. But no one spoke. No one moved to support her. In that moment, she saw with painful clarity that she was already alone.

That night, under the cover of darkness, she packed her few belongings, her battered journal, a single change of clothes, a book she could not bear to leave behind, and left the commune. No goodbyes, no explanations. Just the sound of her own footsteps echoing in the empty streets.

The city stretched before her, indifferent, endless. The once-revolutionary ideas she had clung to now felt like fragile paper, crumbling in her hands. She wandered without direction, the neon lights and concrete landscapes feeling more real than any utopian vision she had entertained. Where once she had seen the world in binaries, oppressors and oppressed, those who upheld power and those who resisted, she now saw only the inexorable pull of human nature. No structure was free from it, no system immune.

The realization settled heavily upon her. It was not capitalism alone that bred exploitation, nor socialism alone that could fix it. It was not the commune or the city, nor academia or activism. It was something deeper, something more insidious, power, the relentless force that shaped every interaction, that whispered in every human heart. There would always be those who justified their control, who draped it in the language of equality or progress, who believed their ends noble enough to excuse their means.

The thought left her drained, as if something vital had been stripped from her. She had spent her life in search of truth, but now the very act of searching felt futile. She leaned against the cold steel railing of a bridge overlooking the river, watching as the water below moved ceaselessly, undeterred by the weight of human ambition.

She wanted to scream, to cry, to demand answers from a world that had none to give her. But in the stillness of the night, there was only silence. The city continued on, oblivious to her disillusionment, its lights burning bright against the void.

For the first time, Silvia had no direction. No certainty. No cause to cling to. And yet, she could not return to what she had left behind. She was untethered, caught between what she had rejected and what she had yet to understand.

With slow, heavy steps, she turned away from the bridge, away from the commune, away from everything she had once believed in. There was nowhere to go, but she kept walking, because that was all she could do.

A Deep Breath

Silvia stood on the bridge as the first light of dawn stretched across the river, the water's surface rippling in endless motion. She had spent the night walking, her mind circling the same questions, the same realizations, the same weight that had grown heavier with each step. The commune, the city, the institutions she had fled, all of them had failed her in some way, but perhaps it was not failure so much as inevitability.

The river moved steadily beneath her, undeterred by the structures built around it, the dams placed in its path. No force sought to contain it forever, only to shape its course, to guide its flow in directions that suited the needs of the world. And yet, no matter how much effort was placed in its control, the river remained its own entity, carving new paths, reshaping the land, defying those who thought they could tame it.

For so long, Silvia had believed that freedom could be found in absolutes: in rejecting capitalism, in embracing radical ideology, in severing herself from the comforts of privilege. She had thought that stepping outside of the system was enough, that the right ideology, the right community, would finally offer her the clarity and certainty she had always craved. But certainty was just another illusion, another attempt to carve the world into neat and manageable shapes, to force something wild and evolving into a framework that could never contain it.

She thought of the commune, of Jonah and Mara, of the way they had twisted their own ideals into a means of consolidating power. She thought of academia, where knowledge had been wielded as a gatekeeping tool rather than a force for liberation. She thought of her family, of their sermons on morality even as they maintained their wealth and influence without guilt. None of these places had given her the truth she had sought, but perhaps the mistake had been in searching for truth as something static, something pure.

Truth was not found in systems or institutions. It was not discovered in rigid ideologies or revolutionary manifestos. It was something messier, something living, something that had to be navigated moment by moment, shaped not by doctrine but by action.

Silvia took a deep breath, inhaling the crisp morning air. She felt lighter, not because she had found the answer, but because she had finally let go of the need for one. She no longer needed to cling to a singular path, to measure herself against impossible ideals, to place faith in leaders who claimed to have solved the great riddle of human existence. The world was not meant to be understood in such simple terms. It was meant to be engaged with, to be questioned, to be shaped, not into perfection, but into something better.

She watched the water slip past, always moving forward. She did not know where she was going next, nor did she need to. What mattered was that she was not standing still. For the first time in a long while, she felt the stirrings of hope, not from finding a perfect path, but from realizing she did not need one. She only needed the willingness to keep going, to keep learning, to keep choosing the next step with intention, even knowing she would never reach an absolute destination.

The weight of her past did not disappear, but it no longer defined her. She had been a daughter of privilege, a student of ideology, an idealist betrayed by reality. Now, she was something else, something still in flux, still forming, but free.

She turned away from the railing and stepped forward, not with the certainty of someone who had found all the answers, but with the resolve of someone who no longer needed them. Whatever lay ahead, she would meet it on her own terms.

Chapter 5

The Search

Silvia moved through the world like a ghost, her presence barely more than a shadow slipping between places, unnoticed and unmoored. She drifted from city to city, taking whatever work she could find, waitressing in diners where no one learned her name, cleaning houses that bore no trace of her passage, tutoring students whose parents never asked about the woman who taught their children. She lived in cheap motels when she could afford them, shared cramped apartments with strangers when necessity demanded, and, on more than one occasion, slept curled in the backseat of her car, wrapped in a coat that once smelled like home.

She spoke little, avoided attachments, and let days blur into one another, convinced that this, at last, was freedom. No longer bound by the gilded expectations of her family, the rigid doctrines of academia, or the suffocating idealism of the commune, she was free to exist without being claimed. She did not have to prove anything to anyone, did not have to take sides, did not have to be anything other than the quiet observer of a world that seemed to demand so much and give so little in return.

But as time stretched, that freedom felt hollow. She had escaped the structures that sought to define her, but in doing so, had severed herself from any sense of meaning. The disillusionment she carried had turned into a kind of weightless numbness, an existence neither grounded nor directed. She had wanted to strip life down to its barest essentials, but what she had not anticipated was how easily one could vanish altogether.

There were moments of clarity, fleeting yet persistent, that whispered she was not truly free, only unmoored. She had traded one set of constraints for another, now bound not by expectations but by the absence of connection, the absence of purpose. The world passed before her in a haze of unremarkable days, each one identical to the last. She had become untethered from privilege, from ideology, from obligation, and yet, in that great shedding, she had lost herself as well.

Stillness in Motion

Then, one evening, when the sky was bruised with the last remnants of twilight, Silvia wandered into a part of the city she did not recognize. She had no destination in mind, no reason for walking other than the need to keep moving, to feel the rhythm of her own footsteps against the pavement as proof that she still existed. And then, in the dim glow of an art studio window, she saw something that stopped her, a canvas filled with color, alive in a way she had not felt in years.

The home studio was small, tucked between a bookstore and a bakery that smelled of warm bread. Inside, the air was thick with the scent of oil paint and turpentine. The walls were crowded with art that pulsed with movement, with light, with something unnamable yet deeply familiar. Silvia stood there, transfixed, until a voice broke the silence.

"You look like someone who's forgotten what it means to see."

She turned to find an older woman watching her, hands stained with paint, eyes sharp with the kind of clarity that only comes from having seen too much of the world and deciding to make something beautiful anyway.

"I used to paint," Silvia admitted before she even knew why she was speaking. The words felt foreign in her mouth, like an echo of someone she had once been.

"Then you should start again," the woman said simply. "Come inside."

And just like that, Silvia stepped forward, into the warmth of the space, into the quiet hum of creation, into something she did not yet have a name for, but which felt, at long last, like a beginning.

The woman introduced herself as Lilia, an artist who had lived in the house for decades. She invited Silvia inside, and Silvia found herself in a space that was both chaotic and harmonious. The walls were covered in paintings and sketches, the shelves filled with books and trinkets. The air smelled of herbs and fresh bread.

Lilia lived simply but not ascetically. She grew her own food, made her own clothes, and created art not for profit but for the joy of it. She had no interest in ideologies or movements, no desire to change the world. She simply lived, her life a quiet rebellion against the noise and greed of modern society.

As Silvia spent time with Lilia, she observed the woman's way of being, unhurried, unburdened by the demands of ambition or validation. She watched how Lilia's days unfolded in a rhythm dictated not by schedules or external pressures but by the slow movement of time itself. Mornings were spent tending to the garden, hands in the earth, coaxing life from soil. Afternoons, she painted, the brush moving across the canvas in strokes unhurried and deliberate, capturing light, movement, and the passage of fleeting moments. Evenings, she read, the quiet turning of pages blending with the rustle of wind through the open windows.

Lilia offered no grand philosophies, no manifestos, only the steady presence of a life lived on one's own terms. And for Silvia, who had spent so much of her existence in pursuit, of knowledge, of justice, of certainty, there was something profoundly disarming about the simplicity of it all. She had never known such quiet, such stillness, unburdened by the ceaseless need to justify one's existence.

One afternoon, as they sat in the shade of a sprawling tree, Silvia found herself asking, "Do you ever wonder if you should be doing more? If you should be out there, making a difference?"

Lilia smiled, her eyes crinkling with something akin to amusement. "Making a difference, how?"

Silvia hesitated. She had spent years believing in movements, in causes, in the grand necessity of fighting for something larger than oneself. And yet, she had also seen how those very movements could become consumed by the same power structures they sought to dismantle. "I don't know," she admitted finally. "Something… bigger."

Lilia set her teacup down, considering the words before responding. "I once thought that too," she said. "That I had to be part of something vast, something that shook the foundations of the world. But then I realized that the world does not change all at once. It changes in small ways, through the kindnesses we offer, the beauty we create, the lives we touch. Some people fight with words, some with action. And some simply choose to live in a way that refuses to be consumed by what is broken."

Silvia was silent, the words settling over her like a weight that was not heavy but grounding.

She stayed with Lilia for days that stretched into weeks, learning the rhythms of a life that did not demand constant proving, constant striving. She learned to cook with what the garden offered, to mend her own clothes, to sit in silence without feeling the need to fill it. She learned that rebellion did not always look like protest, that sometimes it was simply the refusal to live by the dictates of a world that measured worth in terms of productivity and power.

And in that small house, surrounded by color and life, Silvia found herself not seeking answers, but simply allowing herself to be. It was, perhaps, the most radical thing she had ever done.

Time, in Time

Silvia continued spending time with Lilia. At first, she felt awkward and self-conscious, her hands clumsy and her mind restless. But Lilia was patient, guiding her without judgment.

"You don't have to be good at it," Lilia said as Silvia struggled to sketch a flower. "You just have to enjoy it."

Slowly, Silvia began to relax. She found joy in the simple act of planting seeds and watching them grow, in mixing colors on a palette and seeing them come alive on the canvas. She started to cook meals from the vegetables they harvested, savoring the flavors and textures. The act of creation, whether through food, art, or tending to the garden, became a quiet form of healing, an exercise in presence that she had long forgotten.

For the first time in years, Silvia felt present. She wasn't thinking about the past or the future, about the systems she had rejected or the ideologies she had abandoned. She was simply living, moment by moment. The weight of expectation had lifted, and in its place was a stillness she had never known before.

One morning, as she knelt in the garden, her hands covered in earth, she realized how different this labor felt from everything she had done before. There was no competition here, no need to prove anything. The plants did not demand justification for their existence; they simply grew, reaching toward the sun, living because they could. She envied them, their simple certainty, their quiet purpose.

"You're smiling," Lilia observed one afternoon as Silvia worked on a painting of the landscape beyond the garden. The realization startled her. She had not even noticed.

"I suppose I am," Silvia replied. It was not the forced, performative smile of the past, not a reaction to expectation or obligation. It was something else entirely, a quiet, genuine contentment, born not from achievement, but from simply being.

Lilia nodded, as if she had seen it coming. "That's what happens when you stop fighting yourself," she said. "When you stop demanding answers and start living the questions instead."

Silvia considered this, letting the words settle like roots in soil. She had spent so long searching, so long believing she needed a cause, a mission, a grand purpose. But perhaps meaning was not something she had to chase, it was something she could create, moment by moment, in the quiet acts of care, of creation, of connection.

The days continued to pass in a rhythm both new and ancient. Silvia painted without expectation of mastery, she gardened without worry over the harvest, she cooked not out of necessity, but for the sheer pleasure of it. The world outside still existed, still demanded and shouted and grasped, but here, within this small oasis, she found another way to be.

For the first time in her life, she was not running from something. She was simply staying.

Permission To Be

One evening, as they sat on the porch watching the sunset, Silvia asked Lilia how she had found such peace.

"I stopped trying to fix the world," Lilia said. "I realized that the world doesn't need fixing. It just needs people who are willing to live in it honestly."

Silvia thought about this for a long time. She had spent so much of her life searching for answers, for systems and ideologies that could make sense of the chaos. But maybe the answer wasn't in the systems. Maybe it was in the small, quiet moments of living, in the garden, in the art, in the connections between people.

She began to let go of the binary thinking that had governed her life, wealth or poverty, power or powerlessness, capitalism or rejection of all material things. She realized that life wasn't about choosing one extreme or the other, but about finding balance.

In the days that followed, Silvia observed Lilia's way of being with new clarity. She noticed how Lilia gave herself fully to each moment, whether she was kneading bread, sketching a flower, or simply sitting with a cup of tea. There was no rush, no urgency, no striving to be elsewhere. Silvia had always thought of peace as something to be attained, as if it were a goal at the end of a long, arduous journey. But now, she began to understand that peace was not an achievement, it was a practice, an approach to living that was cultivated in the smallest acts of presence.

One afternoon, as they worked in the garden, Lilia handed Silvia a handful of seeds. "Plant these," she said. "Not because they'll change the world, but because they'll grow."

Silvia smiled, kneeling down in the dirt. She pressed the seeds into the soil, covering them gently, feeling the cool earth against her skin. She had spent years fighting, years running, years resisting. But in this moment, she was simply planting. Simply living.

That night, as she lay in bed, listening to the wind move through the trees, Silvia felt something shift inside her. She had believed for so long that meaning had to be grand, that it had to shake the world. But perhaps meaning was not found in movements or manifestos, but in the quiet willingness to be present. To care. To create. To grow.

In the morning, she rose early, stepping outside as the first light of dawn touched the earth. She breathed deeply, the scent of damp soil and blooming flowers filling her lungs. For the first time in her life, she felt no urgency to be anywhere else, to seek anything beyond what was already here.

She was home.

As the days passed, Silvia found herself embracing this newfound existence with a sense of peace she had never known. She painted without worrying about perfection, simply for the joy of bringing color to the canvas. She cooked meals with care, not as a necessity but as an act of devotion to the nourishment of her body and those around her. She listened to the birds in the morning, watched the way the sunlight filtered through the trees, and felt the changing of the seasons as something intimate rather than distant.

She spoke with Lilia about her past, about the ideologies she had chased and the movements she had believed in. Lilia listened without judgment, only nodding when Silvia paused, as if she already knew how the story would end.

"You thought you needed answers," Lilia said one afternoon as they sat in the garden. "But all you needed was permission to be."

Silvia considered this, letting the words settle. Perhaps she had always been waiting for something, a sign, a revelation, a cause to dedicate herself to. But here, in this quiet corner of the world, she realized she did not need to chase meaning. Meaning was already here, woven into the simple moments of tending the earth, of creating without expectation, of being present in a way she had never allowed herself before.

She no longer felt the need to fight, to prove, to justify. Instead, she lived. And in living, she found everything she had been searching for.

Plant More Tomatoes

One morning, as she helped Lilia plant a new row of tomatoes, Silvia felt a surge of gratitude. She didn't have all the answers, but she had found something even more valuable: a way to live.

"Thank you," she said, her voice soft but sincere.

Lilia smiled. "You're welcome, my dear. Now, let's get these tomatoes in the ground before the sun gets too hot."

And so they worked, side by side, their hands in the earth and their hearts at peace.

As they dug, the rhythm of their movements became meditative, the warm scent of the soil mixing with the sweet aroma of the basil growing nearby. Silvia felt the simplicity of the task grounding her, each press of her fingers into the dirt reaffirming her place in the world, not as a crusader against injustice, not as a student seeking knowledge, but as a being engaged in the sacred act of growth.

Between planting, Lilia shared stories, of past harvests, of the seasons' turns, of the resilience required to tend to life with patience rather than control. "Nature doesn't ask for revolution," she mused, patting down the earth around a seedling. "It asks for care."

Silvia listened, absorbing the wisdom not as ideology, but as truth revealed in quiet action. For so long, she had sought meaning in great declarations and grand pursuits. Now, she saw that wisdom lived in the soil, in the slow unfolding of a seed's journey to fruit, in the everyday rituals of tending to something beyond oneself.

When they finally stood, brushing dirt from their hands, Silvia looked out at the rows of young plants, knowing that the work was not merely about sustenance, it was about a way of being, a quiet defiance against a world that demanded urgency. In the stillness of this morning, in the shared labor between them, she felt the fullness of the moment, and she understood at last that peace was not something to be found, but something to be cultivated.

Chapter 6

Stillness

Silvia had never known a presence like Lilia's before. There was something about the older woman's quiet certainty, the way she moved through the world with an ease that neither demanded attention nor sought to shrink away. Unlike the figures Silvia had encountered in her past, her parents, her professors, the leaders of activist groups, Lilia had no need to proclaim her beliefs or assert her influence. She simply existed, steadfast and unwavering, like a great tree that had weathered seasons without complaint.

Silvia found herself drawn into the rhythm of Lilia's life, a life governed not by external expectations but by the natural cycles of the earth and the quiet demands of creation. Mornings were for tending the garden, where the soil was rich and dark beneath Silvia's hands, the scent of damp earth rising in the early light. Afternoons were often spent in the kitchen, kneading dough for bread, chopping vegetables fresh from the garden, or stirring thick, fragrant stews over the stove. In the evenings, they sat by the fire, sometimes speaking, sometimes simply existing in companionable silence.

At first, Silvia was restless. The days seemed to stretch endlessly, unstructured in a way that unnerved her. She had spent so many years chasing meaning, searching for the next cause, the next battle, the next ideology that could explain the world's chaos. To suddenly find herself in a space where there was nothing to fix, nothing to prove, felt unsettling.

Lilia, perceptive as always, noticed.

"You struggle with stillness," she remarked one day, as they pruned the tomato plants together.

Silvia hesitated, her fingers tightening around the stem of a vine. "I suppose I do."

Lilia nodded, neither pushing nor offering platitudes. She merely continued her work, and Silvia found herself grateful for the absence of judgment. It was a rare thing, she realized, to be given space without expectation.

Days passed, then weeks, and Silvia began to feel the edges of her restlessness soften. There was something deeply human about planting seeds and waiting for them to grow, about painting not for an audience but for oneself, about cooking meals to be shared rather than consumed in haste. She had spent years in spaces where words and ideas held supreme importance, where abstract theories shaped the way people lived. But here, in Lilia's world, life was not an intellectual exercise. It was tactile, immediate, bound to the present moment.

It was in one of those quiet moments, as they shelled peas on the porch, that Lilia finally asked the question Silvia had been expecting.

"You don't have to tell me," she said, her voice gentle. "But I sense you've been running from something."

Silvia stared at the small green orbs in her hands, rolling them between her fingers. A part of her wanted to deflect, to change the subject, to brush off the question with a half-hearted excuse. But another part of her, one that had grown weary from years of silence and pretense, felt the pull of honesty.

And so, slowly, she began to speak.

She spoke of her childhood, of the grand house filled with polished furniture and whispered conversations about power and influence. She spoke of her father, a man who measured success in acquisitions and alliances, and of her mother, who had learned to wield charm like a weapon, ensuring their family remained untouchable.

She spoke of her escape, how she had walked away from a life of wealth and certainty, believing that somewhere beyond it, she would find truth. How she had sought refuge in academia, in activism, in intellectual circles that claimed to hold the answers. And yet, how at every turn, she had been met with the same hierarchies, the same hunger for control, only dressed in different clothes.

She spoke of the commune, of the disillusionment that had followed, of the slow realization that even those who claimed to fight for justice were not immune to the seductions of power. She spoke of the emptiness she had felt in the wake of it all, the sense of being untethered, without purpose or direction.

By the time she finished, the sun had dipped low in the sky, casting long shadows across the porch. Lilia, who had listened in silence, placed a steady hand on Silvia's own, grounding her in the present.

"You've been searching for answers outside yourself," Lilia said, her voice steady. "But the answers are within you. You just have to be still enough to hear them."

Silvia looked into Lilia's eyes, expecting to see the same certainty she had encountered in so many others, the certainty of those who believed they knew the truth. But what she saw instead was something quieter, something gentler. There was no arrogance in Lilia's words, no assertion that she had found the way. There was only an invitation.

For the first time in a long while, Silvia felt the weight of expectation lift. Perhaps, she thought, she did not need to have all the answers. Perhaps she did not need to define herself by what she opposed or by what she sought to dismantle.

Perhaps she could simply exist, here, in this moment, in this place, and that would be enough.

And so, as the evening breeze carried the scent of soil and lavender through the air, Silvia allowed herself, for the first time, to be still.

Life Through Creativity

Silvia's days no longer felt like a series of battles. She had spent too long in pursuit of something grand, something that could answer the questions that had plagued her, something that could justify the choices she had made, the sacrifices she had endured. But here, in Lilia's home, in the garden where the earth smelled rich and full, in the small acts of cooking, of painting, of tending to what needed care, she found herself embracing something far simpler: life itself, in its most immediate and unembellished form.

For the first time in a long time, she was not engaged in critique or opposition. She was not standing on a platform, defending a cause. She was not writing, arguing, debating, or trying to dismantle some great, looming system. She was simply present, her hands in the soil, her thoughts unburdened by ideology.

Lilia, ever attuned to the subtle shifts in Silvia's mind, noticed this change before Silvia herself could articulate it.

"You've stopped thinking so much," she observed one afternoon as they worked in the garden, transplanting seedlings into freshly turned earth.

Silvia wiped the sweat from her brow and gave a small laugh. "Maybe," she admitted. "I think I got tired of thinking."

Lilia smiled, tucking a seedling into place. "Thinking has its place. But so does doing."

It was in doing that Silvia found something akin to peace. She threw herself into creation, not as a statement, not as a form of defiance, but simply because it felt good to shape something with her own hands.

At first, it was art. She found an old set of paints in a dusty corner of Lilia's studio and began to experiment, moving the brush across the canvas with no real intention beyond the pleasure of seeing color take shape. She painted the garden, the gnarled branches of the trees in winter, the pale light of dawn stretching across the fields. She painted Lilia's hands, the delicate lines etched into her skin, the way they moved so fluidly through each task, as if they had never once hesitated.

The paintings were not perfect. Some were imbalanced, the colors too bold or too hesitant. Some were muddled, the forms not quite right. But for the first time in her life, Silvia did not measure her work against an external standard. She did not ask if it was good enough. She did not wonder if it served a greater purpose. She simply let herself create.

The garden, too, became a kind of canvas. Lilia taught her how to recognize when the soil was too dry, how to trim back what was overgrown, how to wait, patiently, without expectation, for something to sprout. Silvia found comfort in the routine, in the quiet knowledge that things would grow if given the right conditions.

She thought, sometimes, of her past self, the girl who had sat in lecture halls, feverishly taking notes on theories of justice and change, who had stood in protests, raising her voice until it was hoarse, who had tried to fit herself into movements that had, in the end, failed her. That girl had been determined to change the world, convinced that only through struggle could something better be born.

Now, she was beginning to understand something else: that change was not always a revolution, not always a dismantling of systems or a grand reshaping of society. Sometimes, it was in the smallest, quietest acts. In painting without fear of failure. In planting something and waiting for it to grow. In sharing a meal, in mending a torn shirt instead of discarding it, in listening, truly listening, when someone spoke.

One evening, as Silvia sat on the porch, watching the sky turn from gold to deep blue, she realized she was happy. Not in the way she had once defined happiness, not as accomplishment, not as a sense of mission fulfilled, but in a way that was quiet, steady. She was happy because, for the first time in years, she was not running.

Lilia, who had been watching her, gave a small nod. “You’re settling into yourself,” she said.

Silvia turned to her, curious. “What do you mean?”

“For a long time, you’ve been trying to become something,” Lilia said, her voice thoughtful. “Something different than what you were raised to be. Something worthy. But now, you’re just being.”

Silvia considered this. She thought about all the years she had spent trying to define herself through what she opposed, her rejection of wealth, of power, of privilege, of the corruption she had seen in both her family’s world and the world she had fled to. And she thought about how, in rejecting all of it, she had never truly built something of her own. She had only dismantled.

She looked down at her hands, speckled with dirt from the garden, stained with paint from the canvas she had left unfinished inside. These were the hands of someone who created, not just someone who tore things down.

"Maybe that's enough," she murmured.

Lilia, hearing the thought but not pressing her for explanation, simply nodded.

Silvia turned back to the sky, feeling, for the first time, that she did not need to search for meaning in distant places. It was already here. It had always been here.

She just had to be still enough to see it.

Freedom Beyond Ideology

Silvia had long defined herself by opposition. She had been against capitalism, against patriarchy, against the suffocating corruption she had seen in every institution she had once trusted. Her identity had been shaped not by what she was, but by what she refused to be. Even in her moments of deepest conviction, there had been an underlying restlessness, a ceaseless drive to tear down, to dismantle, to reject. But what had she built? What had she created beyond the ruins of the systems she had abandoned?

One evening, as she sat with Lilia in the quiet glow of twilight, she found herself voicing this thought aloud. "I've spent so much time fighting, resisting, leaving. But I don't know what I'm moving toward. I don't even know what freedom is supposed to look like."

Lilia, who had been peeling an apple with slow, methodical strokes, handed Silvia a slice and considered her words. "You've been looking at freedom as a reaction," she said. "As something that only exists in the absence of control. But real freedom isn't just the rejection of what binds you, it's the space in which you create."

Silvia frowned, turning the thought over in her mind. She had always imagined freedom as a great upheaval, a severing of chains, an exodus from oppression. But what if it was not only about tearing away from something, but about shaping something of her own?

Lilia continued, her voice steady. "The world will always have its systems. There will always be those who hoard wealth and power, those who exploit and control. But if your whole life is spent in opposition to them, then you are still letting them define you. Freedom isn't about standing on the battlefield forever. It's about deciding how to live despite the battles raging around you."

Silvia sat with this truth, feeling it settle into her bones. She thought back to her years in academia, where every discussion had been about what was broken, what was unjust, what had to be destroyed. She had thrown herself into activism, believing that to live meaningfully meant to constantly fight. And when that world had disappointed her, she had sought refuge in a commune, only to find the same power struggles and contradictions she had tried to escape. When she had left, she had stripped herself of material wealth, rejecting even comfort, as if suffering itself could be a form of integrity. But had any of it truly been freedom? Or had she only traded one set of constraints for another?

She looked at Lilia, whose life was neither marked by wealth nor by poverty, neither by the trappings of power nor the martyrdom of deprivation. She had not chosen a side in some ideological war. She had simply chosen to live as she wished, as truthfully as she could, without waiting for the world to grant her permission.

For so long, Silvia had believed she had to make a choice: to stand within the systems of power or to reject them entirely. But Lilia had shown her that there was another way, to exist outside of their control, neither consumed by the pursuit of power nor by the bitterness of opposition.

"You don't have to live in extremes," Lilia said, as if sensing Silvia's thoughts. "You don't have to be rich or poor, powerful or powerless. Freedom isn't found in absolute rejection or absolute belonging. It's in the space in between."

Silvia exhaled slowly, as if something within her had finally given way. "So what does that mean for justice? For change?" she asked. "If we just focus on our own lives, aren't we giving up on making the world better?"

Lilia smiled, shaking her head. "No, my dear. Change doesn't come from exhaustion. It doesn't come from burning yourself out trying to control the world. If you want justice, if you want a better world, then you must be capable of sustaining yourself within it. You must live in a way that reflects what you believe, not just fight against what you don't."

Silvia considered this. She had always thought that justice required relentless struggle, that to be morally righteous meant never resting, never stepping away from the fight. But she had seen where that path led, infighting, disillusionment, movements that consumed themselves in their own contradictions. What if justice was not a war to be won, but a way of being? What if the truest form of opposition was to live well, to create, to refuse to be bent by systems that thrived on despair?

She glanced down at her hands, roughened from working in the garden, streaked with dried paint from an unfinished canvas inside. These were not the hands of a revolutionary in the way she had once imagined. But they were hands that had planted seeds, that had shaped beauty, that had learned to hold without grasping. Was that not its own kind of power?

For the first time, she understood that she was not abandoning the fight for justice. She was simply choosing a different way of waging it, not in protests and slogans, but in the way she lived each day. She would not spend her life consumed by opposition, forever defined by what she stood against. Instead, she would create something, however small, however fleeting, that embodied what she believed in.

Lilia placed a gentle hand on Silvia's shoulder, her voice soft but firm. "You don't need to fix the world. You just need to be someone who lives in it honestly."

Silvia closed her eyes for a moment, feeling something within her settle. She had spent years running, toward something, away from something, but for the first time, she felt no urgency to move. She did not need to seek or to flee. She could simply be.

When she opened her eyes again, the sky had darkened, the first stars beginning to shimmer in the distance. The world had not changed. The injustices she had once railed against still existed. The powerful still held their thrones. The battles still raged. But for the first time, Silvia did not feel trapped between submission and opposition.

She could choose her own path. And that was freedom.

Here

As the evening sun dipped below the horizon, bathing the sky in hues of crimson and amber, Silvia sat on the wooden steps of the porch, her arms wrapped around her knees. The quiet hum of cicadas filled the air, blending with the distant murmur of the river beyond the garden. She had spent many nights here, watching the sky darken, tracing the slow rhythm of the earth settling into twilight. But tonight was different. Tonight, she felt something stirring within her, a realization, an understanding that had eluded her through all the years of searching and striving.

She turned her gaze toward the river, its steady current winding through the landscape, carving its way not through force, but through persistence. She had always thought of resistance as an act of will, a fight against, a refusal to yield. But the river did not fight the land. It did not challenge the rocks in its path, nor did it attempt to break them apart. It flowed around them, shaping itself to the contours of the earth, finding a way forward not through destruction, but through adaptation. It was not weak, nor was it passive. It was simply what it was, constant, unceasing, free.

She had spent so much of her life locked in battle, against her family, against systems of power, against ideology, against herself. Every decision had been a reaction to something, every movement defined by what she was rejecting. But what if she no longer needed to fight? What if freedom was not in resistance, but in movement? What if the truest rebellion was not destruction, but creation?

Silvia exhaled, long and slow, as if releasing the weight she had carried for so long. She had spent years seeking something certain, some grand revelation that would finally make sense of the world. She had believed that meaning could be found in revolution, in rejection, in tearing down the structures that confined her. But perhaps meaning was not something to be found. Perhaps it was something to be lived.

She whispered a promise to herself, barely audible over the rustling leaves. "I will live on my own terms. I will create. I will connect. I will be free."

The words settled in her chest, not as a declaration of war, but as a quiet, steady truth. She would no longer define herself by what she opposed. She would no longer be bound by the fear of complicity, the dread of failing to live up to some imagined standard of moral purity. She would simply exist, not in isolation, not in constant rebellion, but in the fullness of her own being.

She thought of Lilia's quiet wisdom, the way she moved through life without the need for grand gestures or proclamations. She had not abandoned justice, nor had she surrendered to apathy. She had simply chosen to build a life that reflected what she believed, rather than spending her days dismantling the beliefs of others. It was not indifference. It was not resignation. It was a kind of power Silvia had never considered before.

The wind stirred the trees, carrying the scent of damp earth and blooming flowers. Silvia closed her eyes and let it wash over her. She felt weightless, unburdened by the expectations that had once felt so suffocating. For the first time in years, she was not searching. She was not running. She was not trying to mold herself into something worthy of purpose. She was simply here.

She thought of the girl she had been when she left her family's estate, certain that truth could be found in the dismantling of power. She thought of the student who had thrown herself into theory and ideology, believing that justice could be distilled into a doctrine. She thought of the activist who had burned with righteous anger, desperate to change the world. And she thought of the woman who had wandered, untethered and disillusioned, convinced that meaning was a mirage, an illusion that disappeared the moment she reached for it.

She was none of those people anymore. And yet, she carried them all within her, their voices woven into the fabric of her being. She was not rejecting them; she was not erasing them. She was simply allowing them to coexist.

The river flowed, unbothered by its past, unconcerned with where it had been. It moved forward, not because it was forced to, but because that was its nature. And so, too, would she.

She rose from the porch steps, stretching her arms toward the darkening sky, feeling the coolness of the air settle on her skin. The garden stretched before her, the plants swaying gently in the breeze, their roots deep in the soil, their leaves reaching upward, thriving without question. They did not ask whether their existence was meaningful. They did not search for a purpose beyond growth, beyond life itself.

Silvia turned and stepped inside, feeling, for the first time in a long while, that she did not need to know where she was going. The path would unfold as it always had, one step, one breath, one moment at a time.

She was free.

Without a Map

The next morning, the world was bathed in a golden stillness, the kind that only came in the early hours before the day had truly woken. Silvia stood barefoot in the garden, feeling the cool earth beneath her feet, her hands wrapped around a basket of tomato seedlings. Lilia was already kneeling by the plot they had prepared, her fingers working steadily in the soil, coaxing the earth to receive new life. There was something deeply grounding about this moment, about the quiet industry of it, about the way it required no debate, no ideology, no abstraction. Just hands, earth, seed, and time.

Silvia knelt beside her, pressing her fingers into the dirt. The soil was warm from the previous day's sun, rich with the scent of life and decay. Lilia handed her a seedling, its tiny green leaves trembling in the morning breeze.

"Here," she said simply.

Silvia took it, cupping it in her palm as if it were something fragile and precious. She dug a small hole, placing the seedling inside with careful hands, covering its roots with soil, pressing it gently so it would hold firm. She had done this many times before, yet today, the act felt like something more. It was not just planting, it was a continuation, a quiet promise to herself, to the earth, to the life she had not yet fully imagined.

For so long, Silvia had searched for certainty. She had believed that enlightenment was something to be grasped, that meaning was something one could find as one finds a buried relic, whole and complete, waiting to be uncovered. But there were no such artifacts in the soil, no hidden truths waiting to be discovered beneath the surface. There was only the seed, the patience of the gardener, the slow and steady unfolding of life itself.

She looked over at Lilia, who was working without hurry, without hesitation, as if she had done this a thousand times before and would do it a thousand times again. Silvia had spent her life looking for teachers, people who could explain the world, who could offer a map or a doctrine that would make sense of the chaos. But Lilia had never sought to teach her anything. She had simply offered her space to be, to exist without the weight of expectation. It was Silvia who had done the learning, not by absorbing knowledge, but by unlearning the need for grand revelations.

Silvia pressed another seedling into the earth. There was something sacred in the simplicity of the act. Not in the way religion had once framed the sacred, not as an exalted moment separate from the mundane, but in the way it bound her to life, to the quiet labor of creation. She had spent years caught between rebellion and despair, convinced that to live fully, she had to either resist everything or surrender entirely. But now, kneeling in the dirt, she realized there was another way: not resistance, not surrender, but presence.

The work was slow and rhythmic. They moved down the row together, tending to each seedling with careful hands. The morning air was cool against Silvia's skin, but she could already feel the warmth rising with the sun. She thought of the river, of how it had always flowed without asking permission, without seeking justification for its movement. It was not trying to be anything other than what it was.

She was learning to do the same.

As they reached the last of the seedlings, Silvia paused, wiping her hands on her trousers. She turned to Lilia, studying the lines on her face, the ease with which she moved through the world.

"Thank you," Silvia said, her voice quieter than she had intended.

Lilia glanced at her, the corners of her mouth curving in a faint smile. "For what?"

Silvia hesitated, but she knew there was no single answer to the question. Thank you for letting me be. Thank you for not expecting me to be anything other than what I am. Thank you for showing me that I don't need a map.

"For the tomatoes," Silvia said at last.

Lilia laughed, shaking her head. "You planted them, my dear."

Silvia nodded. Yes, she had.

They sat in silence for a while, watching the leaves tremble in the breeze. The garden stretched before them, full of things they had nurtured, things that would take root and grow long after they had finished this morning's work. That was the nature of tending to life, it did not demand grand gestures, only small, steady acts of care.

For so long, Silvia had been searching for a single answer, a singular truth that would anchor her in the world. But she understood now that there was no such thing. There were only moments, of planting, of tending, of watching something grow. The work of being, of creating, of continuing.

She stood, stretching her arms overhead, feeling the quiet pull of her muscles, the grounding weight of her own body. She was here, in the present, in the world, and that was enough.

The morning had already begun to warm, the light filtering through the trees casting dappled shadows on the earth. Silvia looked around, taking in the scene,. Lilia, the rows of seedlings, the distant shimmer of the river. She had no certainty of what lay ahead, no doctrine to guide her steps. But she had her hands in the earth, her breath in her lungs, her feet steady beneath her.

She was ready.

She turned toward the house, Lilia following behind her, their steps slow, unhurried. There was work to be done, of course. There always was. But for now, there was nothing more pressing than the simple act of moving forward.

Not with certainty, but with readiness.

Not with a map, but with trust in the path as it revealed itself.

Silvia smiled to herself, breathing in the morning air. She did not know what came next. But for the first time in her life, that no longer frightened her.

It simply was.

And for now, that was enough.

Chapter 7

Maya's Rise

Years had passed since Silvia had last seen Maya. Their friendship, once a lifeline, had faded into occasional messages and distant memories. But one day, Silvia received a letter, an actual letter, handwritten on thick, expensive paper. It was from Maya.

Silvia,
I've thought of you often over the years. I've followed your journey from afar, and I admire the life you've built. I'm writing to ask for your help. I've entered politics, and I'm running for office. I believe we can make real change from within the system. But I can't do it alone. I need people like you, people who see the cracks and aren't afraid to speak the truth. Will you join me?
With love,
Maya

Silvia read the letter again, the weight of its request settling over her like a thick, unshakable mist. She had not thought of politics in years, not in any real sense. It had once consumed her, the fiery debates, the restless activism, the fervent belief that systems could be dismantled, reimagined, rebuilt into something just. But those years had burned her out, left her hollow and disillusioned. She had walked away not because she did not care, but because she had cared too much, enough to recognize the limits of what she had once thought possible.

Yet here was Maya, still fighting. Still believing.

Silvia set the letter down and stared out at the garden. The tomato plants had begun to bear fruit, their green skins swelling under the summer sun. She thought of the slow, patient labor that had gone into nurturing them, the quiet work of tending, of waiting, of trusting in a process that was neither instant nor certain. It was a different kind of faith, one that had taught her to live, to let go of the need for grand victories in favor of small, steady acts of care.

And yet, something in Maya's words unsettled her. The promise of change from within. Silvia had spent years rejecting that notion, convinced that the system itself was the root of the problem. But what if she had been wrong? Or at least, what if the truth was not so simple?

Lilia found her sitting on the porch later that evening, the letter still in her hands. She said nothing at first, only settled into the chair beside her, the creak of the wood filling the silence between them.

"You look like a woman being pulled in two directions," Lilia said finally.

Silvia exhaled a slow breath. "Maya wants me to help with her campaign."

Lilia raised an eyebrow. "And what do you want?"

"I don't know," Silvia admitted. "I thought I had found peace here. A way to live without being caught in the machinery of it all. But Maya… she still believes in fighting from within. And she thinks she can win."

Lilia nodded, watching the sky darken into deep hues of indigo and violet. "Belief is a powerful thing," she said. "But so is knowing when to step away. The question is, do you miss the fight? Or do you miss Maya?"

Silvia had no answer for that, not yet.

A week later, Silvia boarded a train bound for the city. She had written back to Maya, not with a commitment, but with a quiet promise to listen. To see for herself what her old friend had built, what she was trying to do. The train rocked gently as it moved, the landscape shifting from open fields to the dense sprawl of buildings and streets, a world she had once fled but never entirely left behind.

She found Maya in a campaign office that buzzed with urgency, volunteers on phones, staffers hunched over laptops, the air thick with the nervous energy of an impending election. And then, there she was. Maya. Older, sharper, dressed in crisp navy with a confidence that radiated like a beacon.

For a moment, they simply looked at each other. Then Maya grinned and pulled Silvia into an embrace. "You came."

"I came," Silvia said, and it was both a confirmation and a question.

Maya led her to a small office at the back, away from the noise. The desk was cluttered with notes, schedules, policy drafts, half-finished cups of coffee. Maya sat on the edge of the desk, folding her arms as she studied Silvia. "You think I'm naïve," she said with a smirk.

Silvia sighed, shaking her head. "No. I think you believe in something that I gave up on a long time ago."

Maya tilted her head. "And yet, you're here."

Silvia leaned forward, resting her elbows on her knees. "Tell me why."

Maya's expression grew serious. "Because things are shifting, Silvia. People are fed up. The old ways aren't working, and we have a real chance to build something different. But we can't do it by shouting from the outside. We have to be in the room where the decisions are made. We have to take power, not just demand it."

Silvia studied her, weighing the conviction in her voice. It was not the wide-eyed idealism of their youth. There was steel in Maya now, a hard-earned understanding of how the world worked, and how to work within it.

"But power changes people," Silvia said. "Even the ones who think they're different."

Maya nodded. "It does. But I'm not here to be different. I'm here to win."

Over the next few weeks, Silvia stayed. Not because she was convinced, not because she had fully embraced Maya's vision, but because something inside her had been reignited, a curiosity, a need to see what this fight looked like from the inside. She attended strategy meetings, listened to policy debates, watched as Maya navigated the political landscape with a deftness that was both admirable and alarming.

It was intoxicating, in a way. The sense of momentum, the idea that they were on the precipice of something real. And Maya, Maya was brilliant. She spoke with fire, with conviction, and people listened. They believed in her.

But politics was not merely about belief. Silvia saw the compromises, the quiet negotiations behind closed doors, the concessions that had to be made to keep the machine running. Maya called it pragmatism. Silvia called it something else.

One night, they sat on the campaign office balcony, looking out over the city. Below them, lights flickered in windows, the hum of traffic a steady undercurrent to their conversation.

"You really think you can change things?" Silvia asked.

Maya took a sip of her drink, her gaze unwavering. "I think we can push the needle. And sometimes, that's enough."

Silvia considered that. Maybe it was. Maybe expecting a revolution was too much. Maybe small shifts, incremental gains, were the only way forward.

But then she thought of the commune, of the movements she had once believed in, of the way power had twisted even the most well-intentioned people. And she wondered, how long before Maya became part of the machine she was trying to steer?

And, more urgently, how long before she did?

The election was still weeks away, but Maya's campaign was gaining traction. The opposition grew more aggressive, the attacks more personal. Silvia watched as Maya handled it all with practiced ease, brushing off the slander, meeting fire with fire. She had become a politician in every sense of the word.

One evening, after a particularly grueling debate, Maya found Silvia sitting in the back room, flipping through a stack of campaign materials.

"You look like someone who's trying to decide whether to stay," Maya said, leaning against the doorframe.

Silvia met her gaze. "I just—" She exhaled, searching for the right words. "I don't know if this is where I belong."

Maya nodded, stepping closer. "Then go. But if you stay, stay because you believe in this, not just because of me."

Silvia studied her, searching for the friend she had once known. She was still there, beneath the polish, beneath the rhetoric. But she was also something else now. Something sharper. Something more dangerous.

She stood, pushing the campaign materials aside. "I need to think."

Maya smiled, but there was something sad in it. "Take your time. But not too much."

Silvia left the office, stepping into the night air, the city alive around her. She had spent her life trying to find the right fight. The right way to live, to resist, to be.

She wasn't sure if this was it.

But for the first time in a long time, she wasn't sure it wasn't.

And maybe that was enough. For now.

Disillusionment

Silvia had entered the campaign with measured hope. Though she had long abandoned the idea that change could come from within the system, she had trusted Maya, believing that if anyone could walk the impossible line between power and principle, it was her. Maya had always been fearless, uncompromising, relentless in her pursuit of justice. But now, watching from the inside, Silvia began to see the slow erosion of that clarity, the small concessions that, brick by brick, built the very structures they had once vowed to tear down.

At first, the compromises were subtle, an agreement to soften language on wealth redistribution, a shift in rhetoric to make policy proposals more "palatable" to a broader audience. The campaign meetings, once filled with impassioned debates about justice and systemic change, had become exercises in political calculus. Phrases like "electability," "strategic alliances," and "incremental reform" began to dominate the discussions. Silvia listened as Maya's advisors spoke of the necessity of "meeting people where they are," of "building consensus," of the "political realities" that constrained what was possible.

She recognized the language. It was the same reasoning her father's colleagues had used at their polished dinner parties, where the wealthy spoke of philanthropy while ensuring their own fortunes remained intact. It was the same justifications she had heard in academia, where radical theories were dissected in seminar rooms but never put into practice. And now, she heard it in Maya's campaign, a campaign that had begun as a movement but was slowly morphing into just another machine.

The breaking point came during a strategy meeting, when the discussion turned to fundraising. A key advisor, a man who had once worked for corporate lobbyists but now called himself a progressive strategist, was explaining the necessity of courting large donors.

"We need their support to win," he said, with the air of someone stating an obvious truth. "If we can get them on our side, we'll have the resources to actually implement these policies once Maya is in office."

Silvia, who had been listening in growing disbelief, finally spoke. "But what policies? If we're taking money from the people who profit from inequality, how can we claim to be fighting against it?"

The room fell silent. The advisor glanced at Maya, waiting for her to intervene. When she didn't, he pressed on.

"That's an oversimplification, Silvia. We're not taking money from exploiters, we're making them invest in change. If we shut them out entirely, we'll never have the leverage to challenge their power."

Silvia turned to Maya. "You believe that?"
Maya hesitated for a fraction of a second, long enough for Silvia to see the doubt in her friend's eyes before she buried it beneath the smooth confidence of a politician.

"We have to be pragmatic, Silvia," Maya said finally. "We can't afford to alienate the donors. Politics is about strategy. We need to play the game if we want to change it."

Silvia felt something inside her crack. This was Maya, the same Maya who had once told her that justice couldn't be bought, who had railed against politicians who put profit over principle. And now, here she was, making the same calculations they had once despised.

She leaned forward, her voice steady but sharp. "But what if the game itself can't be changed? What if every step we take to win it just reinforces the system we're supposed to be dismantling?"

Maya's jaw tightened, but she didn't look away. "If we don't play, we lose."

Silvia shook her head. "No. If we play, we've already lost."

The words hung in the air, heavy with unspoken truths. The meeting continued without her. Voices resumed their measured, strategic tones, discussing how best to frame policy to appease the right people. But Silvia wasn't listening anymore. She already knew what she had to do.

That night, she sat alone in her campaign office, staring at the stacks of policy briefs and talking points, the posters with Maya's face emblazoned with the word *CHANGE*. She wanted to believe it wasn't too late, that Maya could still break free, that the system could be bent into something just. But deep down, she knew better.

The system wasn't designed to be reformed. It was designed to absorb those who entered it, to make revolutionaries into pragmatists, to replace ideals with compromises until nothing remained of the original vision except the illusion of progress.

Maya had once been the fiercest person Silvia knew. And yet, even she was being shaped by the very machine they had sworn to dismantle.

Silvia closed her eyes. She could already hear Lilia's voice in her mind, gentle but firm: *You don't have to be defined by what you're against. You can be defined by what you choose to build.*

She exhaled slowly, already knowing what came next.

A Departure

Silvia lingered in the campaign office long after the others had left, the weight of the evening pressing heavily on her shoulders. The posters bearing Maya's image seemed almost accusatory now, the bold, hopeful slogans ringing hollow in her ears. *Change begins here. A future for all. We fight for justice.* But whose justice? And at what cost?

She had seen this cycle before, idealism swallowed by pragmatism, revolutionaries reshaped into reformers, fire dimmed into embers by the slow, grinding machinery of the system. Maya had always been the fiercest among them, the one who had refused to bend, the one who had scoffed at incremental change as the lie that it was. Yet here she was, standing at the same crossroads where so many before her had hesitated, weighing power against principle and finding herself unable to walk away.

Silvia stood, pacing the room, her fingers trailing across the edge of the desk. She knew that Maya believed in what she was doing. She knew that Maya still wanted justice, still wanted to fight for those who had been silenced and forgotten. But she also knew that every compromise made in the name of victory came at a cost, and soon enough, the fight would no longer be about justice, it would be about survival within a broken system, about securing just enough power to stay afloat without ever truly dismantling the forces that kept the world unequal.

And wasn't that the entire point? The system was designed to take the best of them, the brightest, the most impassioned, and mold them into something it could control. It would allow them their righteous anger, so long as that anger could be channeled into something palatable, something fundable, something that wouldn't unsettle the very foundations of power.

Silvia knew what would happen next. If she stayed, she would be expected to make peace with these small betrayals, to tell herself, as Maya surely did, that the end justified the means. That they could afford these compromises now, because later, *later*, they would make it right. But later never came. Later was the language of those who had already surrendered.

She reached for a sheet of paper and a pen. If she tried to explain in person, Maya would argue, would try to persuade her to stay, to see the logic in the strategy they had laid out. And Silvia didn't want to fight with her, not because she feared losing, but because she knew that if she stayed long enough, she might begin to believe it too.

She wrote simply:

Maya—

I cannot do this. Not because I don't believe in you, but because I don't believe in this system. I know you think you can change it from within. Maybe you can. But I cannot. I will always support you, but I cannot be part of this fight, not like this. I hope you understand. There are battles worth fighting, but not all wars can be won on their terms. I choose to walk away not out of defeat, but to find another way, one that does not ask me to become what I oppose.

—Silvia

She folded the letter, left it on Maya's desk, and walked out into the night.

The air was crisp, and for the first time in weeks, she felt like she could breathe. She didn't know where she was going, only that she couldn't stay. She had spent so long trying to find the right path, trying to determine where she belonged, what role she was supposed to play in this vast, unjust world. But maybe there was no singular path. Maybe there was no map, no prescribed journey, no system or ideology that could provide all the answers.

She thought of Lilia, of the quiet, deliberate way she lived, neither detached from the world nor consumed by it. She thought of the garden, of the river, of the way life continued despite the endless cycles of power and corruption. Perhaps, in the end, freedom was not something granted or won, but something chosen. A refusal, not only of oppression, but of the narratives that demanded one must play a role within the machine in order to change it.

She walked on, the city's lights stretching out before her, the weight of expectation finally lifting from her shoulders. She did not know exactly what came next. But for the first time in a long time, she was at peace with that uncertainty.

An Alternative Path

Silvia arrived at Lilia's house just as dusk settled over the garden, the fading light casting long shadows over the rows of tomatoes and lavender. The sight of it, the quiet abundance, the unpretentious beauty, felt like a balm to her weary spirit. She had left Maya's campaign not in anger, nor even in grief, but with the heavy certainty that she no longer belonged in that world. It had been a gradual realization, one that had grown with each compromise, each justification, each moment in which she watched idealism bend beneath the weight of power. Now, standing before Lilia's small house, she felt a deep and unexpected relief.

Lilia was kneeling in the soil when Silvia found her, plucking weeds from between the rows of herbs. Without a word, Silvia dropped to her knees and began to help, the familiar sensation of earth beneath her fingers grounding her, pulling her from the haze of frustration that had accompanied her long drive back. Lilia did not ask questions. She let the silence stretch between them, only breaking it when she deemed it necessary.

"Back so soon?" she finally said, glancing at Silvia with the same steady, knowing gaze she had always had.

Silvia exhaled. "I couldn't do it."

Lilia simply nodded, as if she had known this all along.

They finished their work, moving in quiet companionship, and when they finally sat together on the porch, Lilia poured them each a cup of tea. The steam curled in the cool evening air, and Silvia stared into it as though answers might be found there, swirling between the tiny ripples on the surface.

"I thought I could help," she admitted after a long silence. "I thought maybe Maya was right, that you could work within the system, change it from the inside." She paused, searching for the right words. "But I couldn't stop seeing it for what it was. The game isn't meant to be won, not by people like us. It's designed to wear you down, to make you think you're making progress while pulling you further into its machinery."

Lilia nodded, her expression thoughtful. "And so you left."

Silvia laughed bitterly. "I walked away from everything, my family, my privilege, my education, even the movements that claimed to be about justice. And now this, too. I don't know what that makes me. A coward? A failure?"

Lilia took a slow sip of her tea before answering. "It makes you someone who refuses to be owned. By money. By politics. By ideology. By the need to win." She set her cup down and met Silvia's gaze. "You don't owe the world your exhaustion, Silvia. You don't have to burn yourself to ash to prove that you care."

Silvia looked away, her throat tightening. She had spent so long defining herself by what she was against, by what she rejected, what she resisted, that she had never stopped to consider what she wanted to build. She had thought that freedom was about opposition, about standing firm against the forces of corruption and greed. But what if true freedom was something else entirely? Not just rejecting the brokenness of the world, but creating something different, something that did not require permission from power to exist?

Lilia gestured toward the garden, the small house, the worn wooden porch beneath them. "This is not a rebellion. This is not an ideology. This is just a life."

Silvia let the words settle within her, feeling them take root. She thought of Maya, of the campaign offices filled with strategy meetings and compromises. She thought of her childhood home, with its cold grandeur and its lifeless wealth. She thought of the communes, the activist spaces, the intellectual circles where power had simply worn a different mask. And then she thought of this place, of the dirt beneath her nails, of the scent of basil and rosemary in the air, of the small but steady rhythms that defined each day here.

For so long, she had searched for a way to be in the world that did not demand she surrender herself to something larger. Maybe this was it. Not in grand gestures or sweeping change, but in the quiet, persistent act of living with integrity, outside the noise, outside the machine.

She finished her tea and set the cup down beside Lilia's. "I don't know what's next," she admitted.

"You don't have to," Lilia said. "You just have to live."

And for the first time in her life, Silvia believed that might be enough.

Art for Art's Sake

The evening was quiet, save for the distant hum of cicadas and the occasional rustle of wind through the garden. Silvia stood at the doorway of Lilia's home, watching as the last light of the sun stretched long shadows over the earth. For the first time in years, she felt no urgency, no restless pull toward the next battle, the next movement, the next cause that would demand all of her and give back nothing but exhaustion. She had spent so much of her life searching for meaning in opposition, defining herself by what she refused to accept. And now, in the fading light, she saw a different possibility, not a resignation, but a quiet act of defiance all its own.

She turned back inside and walked to the small room that had become hers, where a blank canvas stood waiting by the window. A paintbrush lay beside it, untouched for weeks. She picked it up, turning it between her fingers, remembering the weight of all the expectations she had once carried. Expectations to fight, to prove, to win. But for whom? And at what cost?

She dipped the brush into a pool of color and brought it to the canvas, letting the first stroke land without thought, without hesitation. It was not meant to be anything other than itself, no grand statement, no political message, no deeper meaning beyond the act of creating. It was a simple movement, a reclaiming of space, of time, of her own presence in the world.

As she worked, she felt the struggle begin to settle within her, not as regrets, but as steps that had led her here. She had not failed, though she had once believed she had. To reject what did not serve her, to walk away from the corruptions of power rather than letting them mold her, was no failure. It was, perhaps, the only true victory.

Lilia passed by the open door, pausing to glance at the canvas. She did not comment on the work itself, nor did she offer praise or critique. She only smiled, a quiet understanding passing between them. Silvia was not painting for approval. She was painting because she wanted to, because she could.

Outside, the sun dipped below the horizon, streaking the sky in deep oranges and purples. Silvia stepped away from the easel and moved to the window, watching the colors shift, their beauty fleeting yet undeniable. There was no permanence in them, no fixed message. They simply were.

She thought of Maya, of the campaign office filled with strategies and calculations, of the endless justifications required to navigate the machinery of power. She thought of the commune, of its hidden hierarchies, of the voices silenced in the name of consensus. She thought of the institutions she had studied, the movements she had joined, the systems she had tried to dismantle.

All of them had failed her in some way, but that did not mean she had failed. She had spent her life trying to bend the world toward something better, only to realize that change did not always come in the form of revolutions or policies. Sometimes, change was quieter. It was the refusal to be owned, to be defined by the very forces she had opposed. It was the choice to step outside of the endless struggle and simply live.

She whispered a promise to herself, not one of grand ambitions or urgent demands, but of something deeper, something truer.

I will live by my own truth, not by the dictates of ideology, power, or expectation.

Her hands, so long clenched in resistance, slowly opened. Not in surrender, but in readiness. In acceptance of what was, and of what could be.

And as the night settled over the earth, Silvia turned back to her canvas, her brush steady, her heart unburdened, ready to create.

For some time the strokes were tentative, unplanned, but as her hand moved, the colors began to flow with a certainty she had not felt in years. The brush glided across the canvas, layering deep blues and streaks of gold, a quiet conversation between herself and the world she had once tried so hard to reshape. She was no longer seeking to impose meaning, she was simply allowing it to emerge.

The act of painting was not unlike planting in Lilia's garden, both required patience, an understanding that growth could not be forced, only tended. Each brushstroke was a seed, not of revolution, but of something more organic: a slow, unfolding truth.

She lost track of time, lost in the rhythm of creation. The room around her faded, and all that remained was the movement of color, the soft rustling of leaves outside, the breath of night settling in. This was not an escape, nor was it an ending. It was a beginning, a quiet reclamation of self.

Lilia's voice broke through the stillness. "Would you like some tea?"

Silvia turned, blinking as she stepped back from the painting. Lilia stood in the doorway, her presence as steady and grounding as ever. There was no urgency in her question, no expectation, only an invitation.

Silvia smiled. “Yes,” she said, setting the brush down. “I would.”

As she followed Lilia into the kitchen, the night stretched wide before her, full of unknowns, full of possibility. She no longer needed a path or a destination. She had let go of the idea that she must be one thing or another, activist or artist, fighter or dreamer, radical or wanderer. She was simply herself, and that was enough.

Tomorrow, she would paint again. She would work in the garden, drink tea in the afternoon sun, and breathe in the life she was building, not as a response to the world’s failures, but as a testament to its quiet, enduring beauty. And that, she realized, was its own kind of revolution.

Chapter 8

Each Act is a Meditation

Silvia returned to Lilia's home with a quiet certainty that she had not known before. The weight of expectation, society's, her family's, even her own, had slipped from her shoulders, leaving her unburdened. She no longer needed to prove herself to anyone. There was no movement to belong to, no ideology to defend, no institution to navigate. There was only the life before her, shaped by her own hands and will, unbound by the demands of a world that had long tried to dictate her purpose.

She settled into the rhythms of self-sufficiency with an ease that surprised her. Mornings were spent tending to the garden, her hands deep in the soil, coaxing life from the earth with the patience she had once lacked. Each small act, pulling weeds, staking tomatoes, watering the tender greens, became a meditation, a silent assertion of her presence in the world. Where once she had fought against power structures and corrupt institutions, now she let her resistance take a different form: the simple, steadfast work of creation.

In the afternoons, she painted. What had once been a source of frustration and self-doubt became something else entirely. She no longer painted with the expectation that her work had to mean something grand, that it had to be profound or revolutionary. She simply painted what was before her, the shifting light on the leaves, the way the wind rippled across the surface of the pond, the imperfect beauty of the vegetables she harvested. And in doing so, she found a quiet confidence, a sense of self that did not require justification.

Cooking, too, became part of the rhythm of her days. She moved through the kitchen with the same mindfulness she carried into the garden and her art. She kneaded dough with strong, steady hands, stirred soups with the ease of someone who understood that nourishment was an act of care, not just for the body but for the soul. There was no rush, no need to measure productivity or accomplishment. Time itself seemed to stretch, to lose its urgency. She found herself no longer checking the clock, no longer feeling the pull of an imagined future that needed her attention.

She was here. She was present.

The simplicity of her life was not one of deprivation but of intention. Each choice was deliberate, free from the distractions and excesses that once consumed her. She did not reject the world, nor did she shut herself away from it, she simply refused to let it own her.

In time, her art began to draw attention. Collectors and gallery owners came looking for her work, drawn to something in the depth of her colors, the stillness captured in her strokes. At first, she was wary. She had seen how success could become its own form of entrapment, how it could turn passion into commodity. But she met each offer with detachment, refusing to let validation shape her work. She sold pieces when it suited her, gave many away, and used the money that came her way to support mutual aid groups, ensuring that her work did not merely circulate in the hands of the wealthy but flowed back into the world in a way that felt right to her.

Lilia, watching from the sidelines, smiled at this transformation. She never spoke of it as a victory, never claimed any credit. She simply watched Silvia grow into the life she had chosen for herself, knowing that some lessons cannot be taught, only lived.

One evening, as Silvia sat on the porch with a cup of tea, watching the sky burn with the colors of sunset, Lilia joined her.

"You've found something, haven't you?" Lilia said, settling into her chair.

Silvia nodded, a soft smile playing at her lips. "Yes," she said simply. "I think I have."

And for the first time in years, she felt no need to explain.

One Step, One Choice

Silvia had never intended to become a guide for others. She had not sought out a role as mentor or teacher, nor had she envisioned her quiet retreat becoming a place of passage for those seeking something beyond the confines of their former lives. Yet, as the seasons passed, her home grew into a sanctuary, a place of rest and renewal for those who, like her, had once been entangled in the unrelenting demands of the world beyond.

They arrived in different ways, some by word of mouth, others drawn inexplicably to the small house with its wild garden, its air of stillness amid the noise of the world. Artists, activists, scholars, and professionals burdened by disillusionment, exhaustion, and a quiet, gnawing grief. They came with the weight of unfulfilled ideals, of battles fought and lost, of dreams reshaped into compromises. And though none of them could quite name what they were looking for, they all shared the same quiet hope, that somewhere, beyond the machinery of the world, there was another way to live.

Silvia did not offer them certainty. She did not claim to have answers, nor did she attempt to prescribe a path. Instead, she did what Lilia had once done for her, she made space. She let them work in the garden if they wished, let them linger in the kitchen as she prepared meals. She let them sit in silence, let them walk through the overgrown fields at dawn, let them breathe in a way they had forgotten was possible. Some stayed for days, others for weeks, and a few, like Silvia herself, left only when they were ready.

One visitor, Clara, arrived in the late autumn, carrying with her a restlessness that had no name. She had spent years in the corporate world, rising through the ranks, securing all the markers of success that had once seemed so essential, salary, status, stability. But she had come to realize that the life she had built did not belong to her. It was not that she despised it, nor that she rejected it with dramatic conviction. It was simply that she had ceased to recognize herself within it.

"I don't know what I'm supposed to do," Clara admitted one evening as she sat across from Silvia at the worn wooden table, her hands wrapped around a steaming cup of tea. "I don't even know what I'm looking for."

Silvia had heard these words before, had spoken them once herself. She did not offer a lecture, did not attempt to convince Clara of anything. Instead, she stood and led her to the garden, where the last of the season's tomatoes hung heavy on the vine.

"Help me with these," Silvia said simply, handing Clara a basket.

At first, Clara moved hesitantly, as though uncertain of what was being asked of her. But soon, her hands found their rhythm, plucking the ripe fruit and placing them in the basket, one by one. The sun was low in the sky, casting a golden light over the garden, and for the first time in months, perhaps years, Clara felt no pressure to be anywhere else.

They worked in silence, and when they had finished, Silvia handed Clara a knife and a cutting board. Together, they stood in the kitchen, slicing the tomatoes, their hands moving with unspoken understanding.

"Sometimes," Silvia said at last, as she placed a handful of basil into the pot, "we think change has to be something drastic. A sudden leap into the unknown. But maybe it's not. Maybe it's just this."

Clara looked up. "This?"

Silvia smiled, stirring the pot. "One step. One choice. A meal shared instead of rushed. A moment of stillness instead of urgency. A different way of moving through the world."

Clara didn't respond immediately, but something in her gaze had softened. The furrow in her brow, the weight in her shoulders, both seemed lighter, if only slightly.

That night, she stayed up writing, her words pouring onto the page in a way they hadn't in years. And when she left the next morning, she did so with a quiet certainty that she could not yet explain.

"You've shown me something I didn't know I needed," she said as she hugged Silvia goodbye. "That it doesn't have to be all or nothing."

Silvia nodded. "You'll find your way."

As Clara walked down the path toward the road, Silvia watched her go, knowing she would never ask whether Clara had made the right choice. The only answer that mattered was the one Clara would come to in her own time.

And so, Silvia's home remained what it had become, a refuge, not in the sense of an escape, but in the sense of a space where one could pause, breathe, and choose a path not dictated by urgency or fear, but by something quieter, something truer.

And for Silvia, that was enough.

Silvia had long since abandoned the need to persuade. Once, she had believed that truth was something to be argued, that conviction required assertion, that those who had seen the flaws in the world had an obligation to pull others into their vision of what ought to be. But life had softened that certainty. Or rather, it had reshaped it, not into passivity, but into a quieter, deeper kind of wisdom. She no longer sought to guide others toward a single truth; instead, she helped them uncover what was already waiting within them.

When people arrived at her home, some lost, some weary, some simply curious, she did not greet them with dogma or declarations. She did not claim to know the answers they sought. She only offered space. A chair by the fire. A mug of tea. The stillness of the garden in the morning light.

Some stayed for an afternoon, sharing their stories in hesitant fragments before departing as suddenly as they had come. Others lingered for weeks, finding themselves drawn into the rhythms of Silvia's life, the slow tending of the earth, the patient work of painting, the quiet hours spent in reflection. There were no obligations here, no demands for loyalty, no requirement to adopt a particular creed. That, Silvia had come to understand, was the problem with so many movements, so many leaders. They demanded devotion in the same way that the systems they opposed had done, believing that change could only come from consensus, from a rigid fidelity to principle. But that was not freedom. That was simply another kind of imprisonment.

"I'm not here to tell you what to do," she often said when a visitor asked for guidance. "I'm here to help you hear yourself."

At first, this answer often frustrated them. People expected certainty, a map, a path they could follow. But Silvia had none to offer, and she did not pretend otherwise. She had learned, through years of searching and disappointment, that no single doctrine could hold the complexity of the world. And so, rather than impose her own beliefs, she let people sit with their questions, their contradictions. She let them feel the discomfort of not knowing.

Some found solace in that silence. Others found it unbearable.

One man, a former activist who had spent years fighting for change only to grow disillusioned by the infighting and stagnation of the movement, stayed for a month. He spent his days chopping wood and mending the roof, his hands restless with the need to work. But at night, he would sit outside, staring at the sky, his expression heavy with thoughts he did not yet know how to name.

One evening, as Silvia joined him on the porch, he sighed and shook his head. "I don't know who I am if I'm not fighting," he admitted. "If I'm not resisting something, then what's left?"

Silvia considered his words for a long moment. "Maybe," she said at last, "it's not about resisting or surrendering. Maybe it's about choosing. Choosing what to build. Choosing how to exist."

The man frowned, as though he had never considered that possibility before. He left two weeks later, still uncertain, but lighter somehow, as if the weight of his own expectations had begun to shift.

Each person who came to Silvia's home left changed in their own way. Some walked away with a renewed sense of purpose. Others left with more questions than they had arrived with. But that, Silvia believed, was as it should be. There were no universal answers, no singular way to live.

And yet, despite her refusal to impose an ideology, despite her rejection of leadership in any conventional sense, people returned. Some sent letters months later, sharing what they had discovered since their time with her. Others came back in person, not because they sought more answers, but because they had come to understand that the search itself was enough.

Silvia remained an anomaly in a world where leaders demanded belief, where movements thrived on certainty, where those who sought change were often expected to align themselves to a singular cause. But she had no desire to be followed, no wish to be turned into a figurehead for some new philosophy.

She had carved out a space where people could exist without being consumed by expectation. Where they could question without fear of punishment. Where they could simply be.

And for Silvia, that was enough.

The Nature of Power

From the quiet sanctuary of her home, Silvia observed the world not with the urgency she had once carried, but with a steady, almost detached awareness. It was not that she no longer cared, on the contrary, she saw everything with sharper clarity. The same cycles repeated themselves, as they always had. Politicians rose to power on promises of reform, only to find themselves ensnared by the very institutions they had vowed to dismantle. Movements swelled with righteous fervor, then fractured under the weight of ego and infighting. There was always some new cause, some new crisis, some new figure who declared that this time would be different. But it never was.

And yet, this no longer filled Silvia with despair. She had spent years railing against these patterns, believing that if people only saw the truth, if they only understood, they would break free. But now she understood: it was not a matter of ignorance. It was simply the nature of things. Power, like the river that wound its way through the valley below, had its own currents, its own relentless pull. It shaped the land, cut through stone, carried away whatever stood in its path. To fight it directly was to exhaust oneself, to be dragged under and lost in the torrent.

One afternoon, as she walked through the garden, a group of visitors sat beneath the shade of the old oak tree, engaged in a debate that Silvia had heard countless times before. They spoke with passion, with conviction, their voices sharp with the certainty of those who still believed in winning. A young man, fresh from university, gestured animatedly as he argued that systems could be reformed, that if only the right people were in charge, true change was possible.

Silvia knelt beside a bed of herbs, plucking a handful of rosemary, and listened without interrupting. When a lull came, one of the visitors turned to her. "Silvia, what do you think?" he asked. "You've seen it all, you've fought for change before. Do you believe it's still possible?"

She straightened, brushing the soil from her hands, and considered the question. They were looking for an argument, a counterpoint to dissect and challenge, but Silvia had long since ceased to engage in such fruitless exercises.

Instead, she said simply, "The system is like a river, it flows where it will. You can't stop it, but you can choose not to be swept away."

A silence settled over them. Some nodded, thoughtful. Others frowned, dissatisfied. The young man who had been so adamant moments before shook his head. "That sounds like giving up," he said.

Silvia only smiled. "Perhaps," she said. "Or perhaps it's choosing where to stand."

She did not press further. Each person had to come to their own understanding, in their own time. Some would leave her home and return to their causes, their fights, their struggles. Others would come to see what she had seen, though they might not admit it even to themselves. It did not matter. She had no need to convince them.

There had been a time when she believed that true peace was found in victory, that to rest was to accept defeat. But she had come to realize that the chase itself was the trap. It was not power that consumed people, but the desire for it, the belief that control was ever truly possible. That was the lie that had kept so many running, fighting, exhausting themselves in a war that had no end.

She had chosen differently.

As the visitors drifted inside for tea, Silvia remained in the garden, breathing in the scent of lavender and damp earth. The river glistened in the distance, winding its way through the hills, carving its path as it always had.

Let it flow, she thought. Let the world do as it will. I will not be carried away.

A Quiet Revolution

Silvia sat on the porch as the sun dipped below the horizon, its final light stretching long and golden over the fields. The evening air was warm, touched with the scent of earth and jasmine. In the distance, the river glowed, reflecting the last rays of the day, its waters moving steadily, indifferently, as they always had. It was a familiar sight, yet tonight it felt different, less like a boundary, more like a promise.

She had spent years trying to change the world, first through rebellion, then through ideology, then through rejection. Each time, she had found herself tangled in the same web of contradictions, power disguised as principle, revolutionaries who became what they despised, causes that were swallowed by the very systems they sought to overthrow. She had walked away from it all, believing for a time that she had abandoned the fight entirely. But here, in the quiet of her home, with the simple rhythms of planting and painting and sharing meals with those who wandered to her doorstep, she understood what she had not before.

She had never stopped resisting.

Her life, as it now was, was its own kind of defiance, a quiet, deliberate refusal to be consumed by the machinery of ambition, of ideology, of control. She had carved out a space where no one dictated her worth, where she did not measure herself against causes or victories. There was no need to posture, no need to persuade or perform. And that, she realized, was the most radical thing of all.

The world demanded urgency. It demanded struggle, grand gestures, and movements that declared themselves in manifestos and marches. It scoffed at small joys, at lives lived outside its gaze, as if only the loud and the visible mattered. But Silvia had seen the cycles of history, had watched how even the noblest movements could be bent, how ideals could be twisted, how revolutions became the next regime. She had seen how people, desperate for something to believe in, surrendered themselves to leaders who promised salvation and systems that offered certainty. And she had seen how easily those promises crumbled under the weight of reality.

Perhaps, she thought, the real revolution was not in tearing down or rebuilding, but in stepping outside entirely.

As the evening deepened, she let her eyes drift over the land she had come to love. The rows of tomatoes were beginning to bear fruit, their vines heavy with the promise of harvest. The wildflowers at the edge of the garden swayed in the wind, their colors soft in the fading light. She had planted these things with her own hands, had watched them take root, grow, and bloom in their own time. They did not demand to be more than they were. They did not seek to prove their worth.

Silvia exhaled slowly, allowing herself to sink into the moment. She had not found certainty, nor did she expect to. But she had found something better, a way of being that was not dictated by systems or expectations. She lived not in opposition to the world, nor in blind acceptance of it, but in the space between. And in that space, she was free.

She whispered a promise to herself, one that did not need validation or witnesses, one that carried no weight beyond the truth of her own heart.

"I will live my life on my own terms. I will create, I will connect, I will be free."

The words settled around her like a hush before the night.

She had once believed that freedom required rejection, that to be truly liberated, she had to renounce every structure, every institution, every force that had sought to shape her. But Lilia had shown her another way. To plant a garden, to make a home, to create art for the sake of creation, these, too, were acts of rebellion. Not the rebellion of fire and upheaval, but of quiet insistence. A refusal to be owned by the world's expectations.

Lilia had never tried to convince Silvia of anything, never handed her doctrine or demanded belief. Instead, she had given her a brush, had handed her seeds, had let her learn through the simple act of doing. And now Silvia saw the lesson for what it was.

To live fully, without seeking permission or approval, was itself a revolution.

The wind carried the scent of damp soil and woodsmoke through the air. In the distance, she could hear the faint murmur of laughter from the house, visitors gathered around the worn wooden table, voices rising and falling with the warmth of shared stories. They would not stay forever. Some would return to their old lives, others would find new paths, but each would carry something of this place with them, a memory, a shift in perspective, the realization that another way was possible.

And that was enough.

The sky deepened to a dusky purple, the stars just beginning to appear, scattered like flecks of silver dust. Silvia stood, stretching, feeling the strength in her body, the steadiness in her breath. She did not know what the next day would bring, nor did she need to. There was bread to bake in the morning, new colors to mix for the painting she had left unfinished. There would be hands in the earth, sunlight on her skin, conversations over tea. Small things, but no less meaningful for their quietness.

She turned toward the house, the warm light spilling from the windows, the life she had chosen waiting for her within.

She was not a leader, not a revolutionary in the way the world defined such things. But she was something else, a woman who had stepped away, who had built a life that belonged only to her, who had found her own meaning in the simple act of being.

The night was quiet, save for the distant hum of cicadas and the rustling of wind through the trees. Inside the house, the murmurs of conversation softened, the warmth of companionship lingering even as silence settled in. Silvia stood for a moment just beyond the doorway, feeling the night air cool against her skin, savoring the hush of the world around her.

She thought again of Maya, of the urgency that had once consumed them both, of the long conversations where they had imagined tearing down the world and building something better in its place. Maya had chosen the path of power, of influence, of strategy and compromise. Silvia had once believed she should do the same. But now she understood, Maya's revolution was not hers to fight. She did not need the weight of office, the validation of victories measured in votes or policies. Her work, her quiet, unremarkable life, was not lesser. It was simply different.

Perhaps all paths led to the same place in the end, not in conquest, not in achievement, but in the steady, daily act of making something worthwhile. A meal, a painting, a garden. A life.

Silvia stepped inside, shutting the door softly behind her, carrying the night's peace with her.

Chapter 9

The Outside

Silvia had grown used to the quiet of her life, to mornings spent in the garden and evenings spent with the slow work of painting, each brushstroke a meditation rather than a declaration. But on this particular morning, the quiet was ruptured by the shrill ring of her phone. It was a sound she had come to associate with urgency, though rarely did it touch her anymore. She hesitated before answering.

"Maya?" she said, her voice tentative.

"Have you seen the news?" Maya's voice was taut, stretched thin with some emotion Silvia could not yet name, fear, anger, or perhaps something deeper, more wounded.

"No," Silvia answered truthfully.

She rarely followed the news these days. It was not out of willful ignorance but because she had long since understood that the world would march on with or without her. The cycles of power, corruption, and collapse repeated themselves, and she had chosen not to be swept along. But something in Maya's voice made her reach for the radio, its static crackling before the voice of the anchor cut through.

"…a scandal of unprecedented scale… decades of corruption, fraud, and financial manipulation exposed in what is being called the downfall of one of the most powerful political dynasties in the country…"

Silvia closed her eyes, exhaling slowly. So, it had finally happened.

Her family's empire, which had loomed so monolithic in her childhood, was crumbling under the weight of its own deceit. It was not a sudden collapse, but rather the inevitable conclusion of a structure built on exploitation, maintained by illusion. For years, they had hidden behind the façade of philanthropy, presenting themselves as noble stewards of wealth and power. But the truth had always been there, lingering beneath the surface, waiting for its reckoning.

She turned the volume up, listening as the broadcast dissected the details. Her father was at the center of it all, his business dealings exposed as fraudulent, his network of political alliances shattered by revelations of bribery, his personal wealth siphoned from the very communities he had claimed to uplift. It was all coming undone in spectacular fashion, the media feeding on the scandal with a mix of feigned outrage and salacious delight.

Maya was still on the line. "Are you okay?" she asked, and Silvia was almost startled by the question.

Was she okay? She was not sure how to answer.

She felt no vindication, no triumph in her father's disgrace. She had no illusions about his nature, nor about the empire he had built. If anything, she felt only a quiet, aching sadness, not for him, but for those who had been harmed along the way. She thought of the people whose labor had sustained her family's wealth, the housekeepers and drivers, the workers in the factories her father had owned, the countless unseen individuals whose lives had been reduced to profit margins in boardroom discussions. She thought of the communities displaced by his ventures, the land he had taken, the resources he had drained.

Silvia had walked away years ago, rejecting the wealth and privilege that had been laid at her feet. But she had never been under the illusion that her departure undid the harm. Leaving did not erase history.

She turned off the radio, the weight of it all settling in.

"It was always going to happen," she said finally. "It was never built to last."

Maya sighed. "Maybe. But I don't think you understand the scale of this. It's not just a scandal, it's the kind of fall that reshapes everything. Your father isn't just being exposed; he's being dismantled. They're coming for everything."

Silvia considered that for a moment. She imagined the family estate, the offices, the boardrooms filled with men who had believed themselves untouchable. She imagined the desperate scrambles to salvage what could still be saved, the shifting alliances, the hushed conversations behind closed doors.

But none of it mattered. She had no desire to witness their downfall, just as she had no desire to defend them. The empire that had shaped her childhood was dissolving, but she had left it long ago.

"I don't need to see it," she said. "It's already over."

Maya was silent for a long time. Then, her voice softer now, she asked, "Do you feel anything?"

Silvia thought about that. She had spent years unlearning the instinct to feel guilt for what she had been born into, but she had never stopped feeling responsibility for what had been done in its name.

"I feel," she said slowly, "that the world will go on."

And with that, she stepped outside, the air crisp with the scent of damp earth, the wind stirring the leaves of the trees she had planted. The radio's static hummed faintly through the window, but she did not turn back. The fall of an empire was only ever a spectacle for those who believed they had something to lose. For everyone else, the world continued, as it always had.

And so would she.

The Machine

The sky was a washed-out grey when Maya arrived, the kind of sky that hung heavy with the promise of rain but withheld its relief. Silvia saw the car before she saw the woman herself, an unremarkable sedan, its engine idling for a moment before shutting off with an air of reluctant finality. And then the door opened, and Maya stepped out.

She looked different. Not in the way time changes a person, but in the way disappointment does. There was something weightier in the way she carried herself, something dimmer in her once-burning eyes. Her clothes, once perfectly tailored, hung just slightly looser, as if the shape of her had shifted in ways imperceptible to the casual observer. But Silvia saw it at once. The sheen of invincibility, of certainty, was gone.

Silvia did not rush to greet her. Instead, she leaned against the porch railing, waiting as Maya crossed the short distance between them. There was no need for pleasantries. When Maya reached the steps, she looked up at Silvia, her lips pressed into a thin line.

"Do you want to come in?" Silvia asked simply.

Maya exhaled, as if she had been holding her breath for miles. "Yes."

Inside, the house smelled of fresh bread and damp wood, of rosemary drying by the window and rain-laden air filtering through the open door. Silvia poured tea without asking if Maya wanted any, knowing that the ritual of it was often more necessary than the drink itself. They sat across from each other at the worn kitchen table, the wood scarred by years of use, of knives chopping vegetables, of paintbrushes left too long to dry. It was a table that had seen far more honest conversation than any mahogany desk in a politician's office.

For a long moment, Maya only stared at the steam curling from her cup. Then, without preamble, she said, "It's over."

Silvia did not ask what she meant. She only waited.

"They've cut me off. The donors, the party leadership, the people who smiled and shook my hand and said they believed in everything I was trying to do. The moment your father's scandal hit, they turned their backs. Not because I was involved, I wasn't, but because I was adjacent. Because I had stood too close to power, and now I reek of its decay."

Silvia tilted her head slightly. "And you're surprised by this?"

Maya let out a sharp breath, half a laugh, half something closer to grief. "No. Yes. I don't know." She dragged a hand through her hair, something she never would have done before, when every strand was carefully in place. "I thought I could make a difference. I thought I could change things from within."

"And now?" Silvia prompted.

Maya looked up at her then, something raw and unguarded in her expression. "Now I don't know if that was ever possible."

Silvia had nothing to say to that. She had known this truth for years, had left the machinery of power behind when she saw how seamlessly it absorbed even the most well-intentioned hands. But she also knew that Maya had needed to learn this for herself. No amount of warning could have made her see what she was not yet ready to accept.

"I spent years convincing myself that the system could be reformed," Maya continued. "That if the right people, honest people, good people, fought hard enough, they could shift its course. But I see it now. Power does not want purity. It does not tolerate it. The moment you challenge its real structure, it ejects you."

Silvia nodded slowly. "You've learned what all revolutionaries eventually do. The system is not broken. It works exactly as it was designed to."

Maya let out a hollow laugh. "That's the most devastating part, isn't it? There was never a flaw to fix. The whole thing is a machine, built to preserve itself."

Silence stretched between them, thick with the weight of realization. Outside, the wind picked up, rustling the trees that lined the garden. Silvia watched as Maya stared into her tea, as if searching for some hidden answer in the depths of the amber liquid.

Finally, Silvia spoke. "Then why not step away? Why not create something outside of it?"

Maya looked at her sharply. "And do what? Just, walk away? Let them win?"

"Win what?" Silvia asked, her voice quiet but unwavering. "What is the prize? Power? Influence? A seat at the table? If the table itself is the problem, what does it matter who sits at it?"

Maya opened her mouth, then closed it again. She had spent so long fighting to hold her ground within the system, to force it to acknowledge her on her terms. The idea of leaving it altogether felt like admitting defeat.

"It's not that simple," she said at last.

"It never is," Silvia agreed. "But staying in the game just because it's the only game you know, is that really the better choice?"

Maya exhaled, shaking her head. "I don't know how to walk away. I've spent my whole life moving toward something. Always planning the next step, the next strategy, the next fight. If I leave this, then what am I?"

Silvia leaned back in her chair, studying the woman before her. She had seen this before, the fear that gripped those who had spent their lives in pursuit of change, only to realize they had been running in circles. The terror of stopping, of having no battle left to define them.

"You're still you," Silvia said finally. "And you still have a choice."

Maya let those words settle. Then, so quietly Silvia barely heard it, she said, "What if I don't know what to do outside of this?"

Silvia hesitated, then reached across the table, her fingers grazing Maya's wrist in a gesture of quiet solidarity. "Then stay here," she said. "For a while. Be still. Let yourself figure it out."

Maya looked at her, the corners of her mouth twitching in something that was not quite a smile, but not quite sadness either. "You always make it sound so simple."

"It isn't," Silvia admitted. "But it's real."

And for the first time in a long time, Maya allowed herself to believe that might be enough.

The System

The days passed slowly in Silvia's quiet world. There was no campaign schedule to keep, no relentless string of meetings, no urgent calls demanding a response. There was only the garden, the morning light filtering through the trees, the rhythmic scrape of the trowel against the soil, the scent of herbs crushed between fingertips. For the first time in what felt like years, Maya had nowhere to be, no crisis to manage, no power to wrestle with or defend.

She had never known such stillness. It unnerved her at first. Her body, accustomed to moving with purpose, now had nowhere to go. Her mind, sharpened by years of strategy and maneuvering, now struggled to find a use for itself. She rose with Silvia in the mornings and followed her into the garden, watching as she bent low over the soil, her hands steady and sure. She helped with the simplest of tasks, pulling weeds, watering the plants, gathering vegetables in a basket worn smooth with time. It was work that did not seek attention, that did not require an audience or validation. It was work that simply was.

Silvia never spoke of the world beyond the house unless Maya did. She did not press, did not question. She only moved through her days as she always had, tending to the small, necessary things of life, cooking, painting, kneading bread, repairing a loose shutter, mending the hem of a well-worn dress. It was an existence so removed from the one Maya had fought for that she sometimes wondered if she had entered an entirely different reality. But in the stillness, in the quiet order of it, she felt something loosen in herself, something that had been clenched tight for years.

One evening, as the fire crackled low and the night air wrapped around them, Maya finally gave voice to the thought that had been circling in her mind since she had arrived.

"Why did you never try?" she asked, staring into the flames. "Why didn't you fight from within the system? If you saw what was wrong, why not work to fix it?"

Silvia, seated across from her, did not answer right away. She held a cup of tea between her hands, her fingers curled around the worn ceramic as if drawing warmth from it. When she finally spoke, her voice was calm, unhurried.

"Because power is like a river," she said. "It doesn't change course for those who fight it. You can't stop it, but you can choose not to be pulled under."

Maya frowned, shaking her head. "But if no one fights, then it continues unchecked. If we all simply step aside, doesn't that mean we're letting it win?"

Silvia tilted her head slightly. "And what does winning mean to you?"

Maya hesitated. The answer that once would have come easily, winning meant passing laws, securing reforms, shifting the course of history, now felt uncertain.

"It means making things better," she said eventually. "It means using power to do good."

"And who controls power?" Silvia asked, setting her cup down. "Who decides what good is? How long does power stay in the hands of those who wield it well before it begins to serve itself instead?"

Maya exhaled sharply, running a hand through her hair. "You make it sound like there's no point in trying."

Silvia shook her head. "Not at all. But fighting power within its own structure is like trying to turn the river back on itself. The structure will outlast you. It will absorb you, wear you down, twist your victories into its own survival. You saw it yourself, how even the best intentions are bent by necessity. You made compromises you once swore you wouldn't. Not because you were weak, but because the system demands it."

Maya looked away. She had indeed made compromises. She had justified them as practical, as necessary. But had they been? Or had she simply been shaped by the structure she had tried to reform, made to fit within it rather than the other way around?

"But walking away feels like giving up," she admitted.

Silvia studied her for a long moment. The fire flickered between them, casting shifting shadows along the walls.

"It isn't," she said finally. "It's just a different kind of fight."

Maya let the words settle. She wanted to argue, wanted to push back, but something in Silvia's certainty made her pause. For years, she had thought of struggle as something loud, something forceful. The speeches, the rallies, the debates. The votes counted and the laws written. She had seen opposition as the only form of resistance. But Silvia had fought in her own way, not by battling power, but by refusing to be shaped by it.

"You think I should leave it all behind?" Maya asked, her voice quieter now.

"I think you should decide what truly matters to you," Silvia replied. "Not what you were taught to value, not what ambition or duty demands of you, but what you, alone, in the quiet of your own heart, know to be true."

Maya looked back at the fire. She thought of the years she had spent chasing change, of the endless cycle of battles, the weight of expectation, the fear of irrelevance if she stepped away. But for the first time, she wondered what it would feel like to stop running.

To simply be.
The following days passed in much the same way as the first. Maya rose early, her body now accustomed to the slower rhythm of life here. She pulled weeds without thinking, stirred the soup without needing direction. And yet, despite the simplicity of it, despite the absence of urgency, she did not feel like she was doing nothing. She was living.

One afternoon, as she knelt in the dirt beside Silvia, she found herself asking, "Do you ever regret it? Not trying to change things?"

Silvia looked up from where she was pressing seeds into the soil. "I do not regret choosing to live as I do," she said. "But I also do not judge those who fight differently. Some are meant for the struggle. Some are meant to build what comes after."

Maya frowned. "And what about those who don't know where they belong?"

Silvia gave a small smile. "Then perhaps their task is to sit with the question for a while."

Maya exhaled, nodding slowly. She was not yet ready to abandon everything she had worked for, but she was beginning to see that power was not the only measure of change. That maybe, just maybe, walking away was not the same as surrender.

It was another way forward.

As the sun began to set, casting the sky in shades of gold and violet, she felt, for the first time in a long while, that she was not being pulled toward some distant goal. She was here. In this moment. And perhaps, that was enough.

Institutions

The days in Silvia's quiet world passed as if time itself had softened. The crisp urgency of Maya's former life dulled against the slow rhythm of this place, where the sky dictated the day's work and the earth demanded patience rather than strategy. At first, Maya found it unsettling, the absence of schedules, of meetings, of the constant forward motion she had once believed to be the very essence of progress. She had spent years waking up with a mission, a battle to fight, a goal to achieve. And now, there was only the garden, the fire in the evenings, the books lining Silvia's shelves.

Each morning, she woke to the sound of birdsong, her body aching from unfamiliar labor. She pulled weeds with her hands, their roots buried deep in the soil, stubborn and unyielding, until, with the right angle, the right patience, they came free. She found a strange satisfaction in it, in the way nature did not bend to urgency, in the way it yielded only when approached with care. She had spent her life trying to force change, to command it through sheer will, and yet here, in Silvia's world, she saw how growth happened not through conquest but through persistence.

"Keep the roots intact if you can," Silvia advised one morning as they worked side by side. "If you rip them out carelessly, they'll only come back stronger."
Maya looked down at the clump of weeds in her hands, their tangled roots still clutching the dirt. She thought of the institutions she had fought against, the cycles of corruption

and power she had tried to dismantle. How often had she believed a victory was final, only to watch the same problems resurface in new forms?

She placed the weeds into the pile and nodded. "I see what you mean."

Silvia only smiled.

In the afternoons, Maya read. She pulled books from Silvia's collection, volumes she had once pored over as a student, as an activist, as a politician. She revisited the words of revolutionaries, the architects of great social upheavals, Marx, Gramsci, Fanon, bell hooks, and Luxemburg. She had once found fire in their pages, clarity in their calls to action. But now, she saw something else: the weight of time upon their ideas, the way even the most radical movements had been absorbed, repackaged, their edges dulled by the very structures they had sought to dismantle.

She read of revolutions that had begun in righteous fury and ended in bureaucracy, of leaders who had spoken of justice and found themselves trapped in the very power they had sworn to challenge. She thought of her own years in politics, the speeches, the carefully crafted messaging, the necessary concessions. Was it all inevitable? Did the nature of power itself corrupt, or had they simply placed their faith in the wrong battles?

One afternoon, she sat beneath a tree with a book open in her lap, though she was no longer reading. Silvia sat nearby, darning a tear in an old shirt, her hands moving steadily. The simplicity of the act struck Maya. It was not grand, it would not be recorded in history books, but it was real. It was a form of care that required no validation beyond its own quiet necessity.

"Do you ever miss it?" Maya asked.

Silvia did not look up. "Miss what?"

"Being in the fight. The urgency of it. The belief that you could make a difference."

Silvia finished a stitch and knotted the thread. "I think I make a difference," she said. "Just not in a way that the world recognizes."

Maya thought about this long after the sun had set.
At night, they talked, not of politics, not of policy, but of life. Of art, of memory, of the way the stars looked brighter when the world was quiet. Silvia did not offer advice, did not push Maya toward any particular path. She only asked questions, gentle and unassuming, questions that dug deeper than rhetoric ever had.

"Do you believe in legacy?" Silvia asked one evening as they sat by the fire.

Maya exhaled. "I used to. I thought that was the point of it all, to leave something behind that mattered."

"And now?"

Maya hesitated. "Now I wonder if it's all just vanity. If we build things only so we don't have to face our own impermanence."

Silvia nodded, tossing a twig into the fire, watching as it curled into embers. "Maybe. Or maybe we create because it's what we're meant to do. Not to be remembered, but simply because we must."

Maya did not know how to respond. She had spent so long trying to carve her name into the world, to leave an imprint that would last beyond her own time. But Silvia, with her garden, her paintings, her quiet way of existing, had built something just as lasting, without needing it to be known. One evening, as the sky turned to gold and the air carried the first chill of autumn, Maya found herself staring at her hands. They were rougher now, lined with the work she had done in the garden. She thought of all the hands that had come before hers, hands that had written, that had built, that had torn down and rebuilt. Hands that had fought, that had held power, that had let it slip away.

"I thought I was fighting the system," she said at last, her voice almost a whisper. "But I was just another piece on its board."

Silvia looked at her, her expression unreadable. And then, with the quiet certainty that had come to define her, she said, "Now you see the real battle. It's not against them. It's within yourself."

Maya let out a breath she hadn't realized she was holding.

For so long, she had thought of herself as a warrior, as someone who had to fight, to struggle, to push against the weight of the world. But maybe that was only another kind of entrapment. Maybe the fight was not about winning, but about choosing where to place her energy. About deciding what was worth carrying, and what was worth setting down.

She did not know what her next step would be. For the first time in her life, she was not rushing toward an answer.

And for the first time, she was not afraid to stop and decide.

Maya stood by her car, the weight of parting pressing upon her. The sun hung low in the sky, casting long shadows across the garden, the house, the quiet world Silvia had built. There was something unnervingly peaceful about it, a stillness that Maya had never quite learned how to carry within herself. She had spent so long moving forward, reaching toward something just beyond her grasp, that now, in the presence of someone who had ceased to chase, she felt unmoored.

She turned to Silvia, her voice soft but certain. "Thank you," she said, "for showing me another way."

Silvia did not answer with words, only nodded. There was no need for grand farewells, for speeches, for promises of future meetings. Maya's path was her own now. Silvia knew that, just as she knew that nothing she had done had been about showing anyone a way. She had merely lived, and Maya had seen.

Maya hesitated for a moment longer, then opened the car door and slid inside. The engine rumbled to life, foreign and mechanical in this place of birdsong and rustling leaves. Silvia stepped back as the tires crunched against the gravel, the car rolling slowly down the dirt road. She watched as it grew smaller, as it turned a bend and disappeared beyond the horizon.

She did not need to know where Maya was going. It was hers to decide now. And that was enough.

As the sound of the car faded, Silvia turned back toward the house, toward the garden, toward the work that was always waiting, steady and patient. There was no urgency in it; no battle cry, no sense of grand importance. She picked up the basket she had left beside the rosemary bush and resumed plucking the last of the ripe tomatoes from their vines.

She was not resisting anything. She was simply living.

Yet as she moved, as she let the cool soil slip through her fingers, as she listened to the hush of the wind through the trees, she understood something with quiet certainty: this was its own kind of revolution. Not the kind that seized power, not the kind that sought to overthrow, but the kind that refused to be owned.

She thought of all the movements she had seen rise and fall, the leaders who had spoken of justice, only to be swallowed by the very systems they had sworn to dismantle. She thought of the endless cycle of corruption and renewal, of history repeating itself in different names, different faces. The world had always been this way, and it always would be. Power did not break; it merely reshaped itself.

But she was not part of that cycle anymore.

She was no longer caught in the machinery of revolt or compromise, of winning or losing. She had stepped outside it, not in surrender, but in defiance of its premise. The battle had never been against a single system or ideology. It had always been about something deeper, the question of whether one allowed oneself to be shaped by the forces of power, or whether one chose to live in a way that those forces could not touch.

She knelt in the dirt, pressing seeds into the earth. The wind was shifting, the sky beginning its slow descent into dusk. She did not wonder what tomorrow would bring; tomorrow would come as it always had, indifferent and inevitable. The world would go on, corrupt, hungry, self-perpetuating.

But here, in this small, unremarkable place, something else was growing.

Chapter 10

The Rise and Fall

From the quiet sanctuary of her home, Silvia watched the world as it ebbed and flowed, the tide of history repeating itself in different faces, different voices, but always the same shape. The past did not vanish, it merely dressed itself in new garments, wore fresh masks, and called itself progress.

She no longer followed the news with the fervor she once had, no longer scoured headlines for glimpses of hope or change. She had learned that the world spun according to its own rhythm, indifferent to the urgency of those who sought to mold it. But still, every now and then, a name would reach her, a speech would drift through the airwaves, a movement would emerge, and she would feel a flicker of recognition, not of hope, but of inevitability.

Reda was the name on every tongue now. A young leader, full of fire, his speeches crackling with passion, his words promising transformation. His rallies filled city squares, his followers devoted, their faces alight with the conviction that this time would be different. Silvia had heard such promises before, seen such men before, felt the pull of their certainty in her youth. Now, she only listened with quiet understanding, recognizing not only the sincerity in his voice but also the machinery that would turn against him in time.

"He's going to change things," the people whispered. "He's not like the others. He won't compromise. He won't bend."

And perhaps, in his heart, Reda believed that too.

Silvia sat on the porch one evening, the air warm with the last breath of summer, the scent of the garden drifting around her.

Lilia was beside her, a book in her lap, though she was not reading. They both had turned their attention to the radio, to the clipped voice of the broadcaster recounting Reda's latest speech.

"He reminds me of Maya," Lilia murmured at last.

Silvia nodded. "He does."

They listened a while longer, the speech building to its crescendo, the crowd's cheers crackling through the static. There was something stirring about it still, even to Silvia, even after everything. He was young. He believed what he said. That much was clear.

And yet.

"They'll break him," Lilia said after a long silence.

Silvia sighed, setting down her tea. "Or he'll break himself."

That was the way of it, after all. The system could not be fought from within. She had seen it again and again, idealists stepping into the machine, believing they could wield its levers for justice, only to find themselves shaped by its gears, their edges smoothed, their principles chipped away in the name of pragmatism. Or, if they resisted, if they truly refused to yield, the system simply ejected them, cast them aside like a body expelling a foreign object.

Maya had learned this lesson, but it had cost her years to understand it. How long would it take Reda?

Silvia did not watch his rise with cynicism, nor with hope. She simply observed, knowing the pattern before it played out. She remembered Maya's voice, weary in the wake of disillusionment: *The system is too broken. It's not built to change.*

Reda did not know that yet.

Perhaps he would be one of the few who refused to bend, who remained unyielding even as the weight of expectation and opposition pressed upon him. But Silvia knew that the system had ways of dealing with those it could not tame. They would smear him, undermine him, paint him as naïve or dangerous, turn the people against him until even those who had once cheered his name questioned his motives. And if that failed, there were always more final measures.

She had seen it before. She would see it again.

And still, despite herself, despite her certainty of how the story would unfold, she felt a small, distant hope. Not that Reda would succeed, she had abandoned such illusions, but that he would learn before it destroyed him. That he would see the truth before the machine ground him into dust. That he would step away while he still could.

She turned off the radio as the speech ended, the noise giving way to the gentle hum of crickets, the rustle of wind through the trees. Lilia exhaled, closing her book as she gazed out into the dusk.

"You still want to believe in them," she said, not unkindly.

Silvia did not answer immediately. She tilted her head toward the sky, where the first stars had begun to appear, faint pinpricks of light against the darkening blue.

"I want to believe they'll see through it before it's too late," she admitted. "That they'll realize they were never meant to win in that arena. That they'll walk away before it devours them."

Lilia hummed in quiet agreement, standing and stretching, her joints cracking. "Maybe he will. Maybe he won't. But the next one will come after him. And another after that."

Silvia smiled, though there was no joy in it. "Yes. They always do."

The world would keep turning. There would always be another Reda. Another Maya. Another leader full of promise and fire, certain that this time, things would be different.

And perhaps, in some small way, things would be. But the river of power flowed as it always had, carving its path through history, reshaping itself to fit the needs of those who wielded it.

Silvia did not fight against its current anymore. But she still watched. Not with despair. Not with hope. Just with understanding.

The garden was quiet around her, the soil cool beneath her hands as she knelt to pull a few stubborn weeds. She had chosen her path long ago, chosen to step away from the noise, from the spectacle, from the endless cycles of rise and fall.

She had chosen a different kind of life.

And she would not trade it for anything.

Acceptance

With the passing years, Silvia had come to accept the nature of power, that it was neither virtuous nor wicked, but only a force, a tide that shaped the world in ways both seen and unseen. She no longer held the belief that systems could be overturned, restructured, or reformed into something pure, something untarnished by greed and self-interest. No, she had seen too much, had watched the rise and fall of men and women who once stood against corruption only to find themselves trapped within its machinery.

Once, she had felt anger at this realization. She had grieved for what she had believed in, for the years she had spent fighting against forces that would not yield. But now, the anger had settled into understanding, the grief into something more resolute. She no longer sought to break the cycle. Instead, she observed it, as one observes the shifting of the seasons, knowing that spring would bring new hope, that summer would nourish it, that autumn would test it, and that winter would come, as it always did, to bury what had grown beneath its heavy silence. And then, inevitably, it would all begin again.

One evening, as she sat in the garden, a small group of visitors had gathered. They were young, some artists, some activists, all carrying the weight of their own disillusionments. They had come to her not because she had answers, but because they sensed she had ceased to ask the questions that tormented them.

"How can you bear it?" one of them, a woman named Elise, asked. Her voice was tight with frustration. "How can you sit here and watch it all happen? The world is burning, and you just sit in your garden?"

Silvia did not answer right away. She let the evening settle around them, let the sound of the crickets swell in the silence.

Finally, she said, "Have you ever watched a river?"

Elise frowned. "Of course."

"And have you ever tried to stop one?"

There was a pause.

"You can't," Silvia continued. "You can build dams, but the water finds its way. You can reroute it, but it will carve new paths. Power is like that river. It shapes the land, but it cannot be tamed. You can fight against the current, or you can step out of it."

Elise shook her head, restless, unconvinced. "So you're saying we should do nothing?"

Silvia smiled, but there was no condescension in it, only patience. "I am saying that you must decide what it is you seek. If you wish to fight, then fight. But know that you are not fighting to win, you are fighting to resist being swallowed. And if that is the battle you choose, then you must decide how long you are willing to endure it, and what it will cost you."

A young man sitting beside Elise, Lucas, ran his fingers through his hair and exhaled sharply. "But if we step out of the river, aren't we just letting it take everything with it? Aren't we just letting it win?"

Silvia tilted her head. "Win what?"

Lucas hesitated.

"What is it that you think must be won?" she pressed, her voice gentle. "Do you believe that if you fight long enough, you will find a world without power, without greed, without the forces that have governed humanity for centuries?"

He looked down, but he did not answer.

Silvia sighed, not in impatience but in something close to sorrow. "It is not the struggle that troubles you, Lucas. It is the fear that it will never end."

The group fell silent. Some stared at the ground, others into the darkening sky.

And then, after a long pause, a voice, softer, quieter. It was Clara, a woman who had once spent her life in protest, who had given years to the cause of justice only to see the movement she loved fracture beneath the weight of its own contradictions.

"But if we do not fight," she murmured, "who will?"

Silvia considered this for a moment, then nodded. "Some must fight. Some must push against the tide. And I do not begrudge them their struggle. But you must ask yourself, are you fighting to move the world, or are you fighting to keep yourself from drowning?"

Elise opened her mouth, then closed it again. Her face was tight with emotion, but Silvia could not tell whether it was anger or grief. Perhaps both.

They sat for a while longer, the weight of the conversation settling over them. Then, slowly, the tension in the air eased. Someone picked up a cup of tea. Someone else leaned back in their chair, exhaling. The fire crackled between them, and the crickets continued their song.

No one had found an answer that night. But perhaps they had begun to ask the right questions.

The next morning, Silvia rose early and went to the garden. The air was cool, the earth damp beneath her fingers as she pulled weeds from between the rows of tomatoes. She had no doubt that Elise and Lucas and the others would leave, that they would return to their lives, their causes, their battles. Some of them would carry on the fight, others would burn out. Some, perhaps, would return one day, older, heavier with the weight of their own disillusionments.

She did not judge them. It was their path to walk. She had walked it once herself.

But she had stepped away. Not in surrender, not in defeat, but in recognition of a truth she had come to understand: that the world did not need saving in the way she had once believed.

The world would move as it always had. Empires would rise, and they would fall. Movements would begin with fire and end in ash. Leaders would step forward, their voices strong, only to be swallowed by the same forces that had shaped those before them.

But here, in this small piece of earth, there was another way.

She pressed a seed into the ground, covering it gently with soil.

The world would go on.

But so would she.

For Truth

Silvia had long ceased searching for answers beyond the quiet life she had chosen. She no longer measured herself against the ambitions of others, nor did she feel the weight of external expectations pressing upon her as they once had. Each day was its own, neither dictated by grand aspirations nor haunted by past regrets. It was not a life that could be easily explained to those who still saw the world through the lens of struggle, but it was one she had come to understand deeply.

She spent her mornings tending the garden, the afternoons painting or reading, the evenings sitting by the fire, speaking in measured tones to those who sought her out. People came and went, seekers, wanderers, the disillusioned and the weary. Some stayed for a night, some for weeks, but none left unchanged. She did not claim to guide them, nor did she offer solutions, only space, space to breathe, to unlearn, to listen to the quiet voice within themselves that had so long been drowned out by the noise of the world.

It was in this way that Diego arrived, his presence hesitant yet eager, his eyes carrying the restless energy of a man searching for something he could not name.

"I heard about you from Clara," he said, standing at her doorstep, his fingers twisting anxiously in his pockets. "She said you, she said you helped her see things differently."

Silvia merely nodded and stepped aside to let him in. She did not ask what he was searching for. People came with their own burdens, and she had learned that they would reveal them in time, or not at all. It was not her role to demand.

Diego settled into the rhythm of the house in the way many did, first with uncertainty, then with quiet wonder at the simplicity of life within its walls. He watched Silvia as she moved through her days, not with urgency, but with deliberate ease, as if each action was as important as the last, and none more significant than the next.

One evening, as the fire flickered low and the sound of crickets hummed through the open window, Diego finally asked the question that had been resting on his tongue.

"How do you do it?" he asked, his voice thick with frustration. "How do you stay true to yourself? How do you not get caught up in, everything?"

Silvia tilted her head slightly, considering him, considering the weight of his question. Then, as if it were the simplest thing in the world, she answered.

"By knowing that my worth is not determined by the world's approval. By creating for joy, not for validation. And by choosing to be around those who value truth over success."

Diego exhaled sharply, as if the answer pained him. "That's easy for you to say."

She smiled, though not unkindly. "No, it isn't."

He frowned. "Then how did you get here? How did you—" He gestured vaguely around the room, toward the paintings, the books, the unhurried peace of it all. "How did you build this kind of life?"

Silvia set down her tea. "By letting go of the need to prove anything," she said simply. "I spent years trying to define myself by what I rejected, by what I fought against, by the ideologies I abandoned. And then I realized that the truest life is not defined by opposition, but by creation. By choosing, each day, what you will make, what you will nurture, and what you will leave behind."

Diego looked away, staring into the fire. "But how do you know it's enough?"

Silvia let out a quiet breath, leaning back into her chair. "Enough for whom?" she asked.

Diego did not answer.

For several days after that conversation, he did not speak of it again, but Silvia noticed the way his presence began to shift. He no longer hovered at the edge of the garden but moved among it, his hands in the soil, his body engaged in the work of planting, of tending, of understanding the patience required to see something grow. He did not just watch Silvia paint, he picked up a brush himself, hesitantly at first, then with more confidence, more freedom.

One afternoon, as they worked side by side, Diego broke the silence.

“I always thought I needed to prove something,” he said. “To show people that I could be great. That I could make something that mattered.”

Silvia wiped her hands on her apron, watching as he traced absent patterns in the dirt with his fingertips.

“And do you still believe that?” she asked.

He hesitated. “I don’t know,” he admitted. “But I think, I think I want to create for myself, not for an audience. I want to stop trying to make something important and just…make.”

Silvia smiled. “Then you’re already free,” she said.

Diego stayed for a few more weeks. He did not speak as often of the world outside, of the expectations and pressures that had once governed his thoughts. He spent his time painting, walking along the river, preparing meals with Silvia and Lilia in quiet companionship. He still carried restlessness within him, but it was no longer the kind that threatened to consume him. It was the restlessness of someone who had glimpsed a different way of being but had not yet fully stepped into it.

When he finally prepared to leave, he did so with no grand declarations, no promises of what he would do next. He only pressed Silvia’s hand in his and murmured a quiet thank you.

“For what?” Silvia asked.

“For reminding me that I don’t have to prove anything,” he said.

She only nodded. “You never did.”

And with that, Diego turned and walked down the path, his figure small against the vastness of the landscape. Silvia watched until he disappeared from view, then turned back to the house, to the garden, to the work that would continue long after he was gone.

She did not know what path he would take, nor did she need to. It was his to walk, just as hers was her own.

She lifted her brush and dipped it into color, pressing it to canvas with the quiet knowledge that she was exactly where she was meant to be.

Revolution of Presence

The evening settled gently over the garden, the sky painted in soft hues of amber and violet, as if the earth itself had exhaled after a long day's labor. Silvia sat upon the wooden bench at the edge of the field, her hands resting idly in her lap, her eyes tracing the horizon where the last light of the sun kissed the land. The air was thick with the scent of earth, of ripened fruit and freshly cut herbs. It was a familiar scent, one that carried with it the weight of a thousand days spent in quiet labor, of seeds pressed into soil and roots taking hold beneath her fingers.

She did not think, in that moment, of the wealth she had left behind. She no longer carried the burden of her father's empire or the shame of its inevitable collapse. The fall of men like him had become little more than another story in the endless cycle of power and ruin, a tale she no longer felt compelled to follow. The world had chewed up his legacy, spit it out, and moved on to its next distraction, its next rising figure promising change, its next scandal to dissect.

Silvia had long stopped reading the news. She knew without needing to see the headlines that the cycle would go on. Power was not truly lost, only exchanged from one hand to another, a current that swept through history with ruthless inevitability. Once, this knowledge had filled her with despair, now, it only deepened her resolve. She had spent her youth believing that to change the world, one must rise above it, that the only way to matter was to seize something greater, to carve a space in the grand discourse of history. But she had seen what happened to those who tried.

Maya had believed in the power of institutions, in the ability to shape them from within, only to find herself broken by their machinery. Others had placed faith in revolution, only to become the very thing they had sought to overthrow. Silvia had walked among them, had watched them fight, had tried for a time to stand with them. But she had also watched them bend, compromise, and be consumed. The ideals that had once set them apart became nothing more than the slogans of a different kind of authority.

And yet, Silvia no longer resented them for it. She understood now that the desire for change was not enough to withstand the weight of the world's expectations. There were those who fought, those who ruled, and those who were swallowed whole by the tides of history. And then there were those who stepped away, not out of cowardice, but out of a refusal to be defined by the very systems they opposed.

She had chosen that path, not a rejection of struggle, but a redefinition of what it meant to resist. Not through speeches, nor policies, nor movements that demanded sacrifice upon sacrifice. But through presence. Through a life lived deliberately, not in opposition, but in quiet creation.

The wind rustled through the trees, and she closed her eyes for a moment, letting the night settle around her.

She had spent years searching for meaning in opposition, believing that truth must be won through struggle. But now, she found it in the smallest of acts, the planting of a seed, the stroke of a paintbrush, the breaking of bread with those who came seeking refuge from the world's demands. Each quiet moment was its own defiance, its own testament to a life that could exist beyond the hunger for power and validation.

She whispered to herself, so softly that even the wind could barely catch it:

"I will live my life on my own terms. I will create. I will connect. I will be free."

With that, she rose from the bench and turned toward the house. Lilia's light still flickered in the window, the old woman reading by the glow of a single lamp, the steady rhythm of her existence a comfort in the growing dark. The world beyond this place would continue its restless cycles, rising and falling, fighting and failing. It would call upon its citizens to pledge their loyalties, to invest in its ideologies, to chase the illusion of victory in a battle that had no end.

But here, in this small corner of the earth, something else had taken root.

A revolution not of protest, but of presence. Not in the seizure of power, but in the refusal to be owned by it.

Silvia stepped inside, the warmth of the house embracing her as the night pressed in around them. She did not know what lay ahead, nor did she seek to. The path was not a straight line, nor was it meant to be. It was a series of choices, made each day in quiet defiance of a world that sought to dictate the terms of her existence.

She had once believed she was running away. But now, she understood: she had never been running.

She had only been walking home.

The night deepened, wrapping the world in quiet shadows. Silvia stood for a moment in the doorway, watching the darkness settle over the fields. The faint outline of the garden was still visible, the shapes of vines and trees swaying gently in the wind. She had spent so many nights like this, standing at the threshold between solitude and the world beyond, knowing that she could step back into it at any time but choosing, again and again, to remain here.

She thought of the people who had passed through her home, those who had come searching for something they could not name. Some had stayed for days, others for months, their hands finding solace in the soil, their hearts steadying in the slow rhythm of life outside ambition. She did not claim to have given them answers, only space to breathe, to remember themselves. And that, perhaps, was enough.

She glanced at the canvas resting on the easel by the window. A painting half-finished, colors blending into something unexpected. It was like everything else in her life, not complete, not meant to be, but simply in motion. She picked up the brush, pressed it to the canvas, and let the night carry her forward.

Conclusion

A Future Beyond Power

The world that Silvia had once sought to reform had not changed, not in the ways she had once believed it could. Power had shifted hands, new leaders had emerged, movements had risen and fractured, but the machinery of the system remained largely intact. It absorbed its critics, repackaged its failures as progress, and found new ways to convince the disillusioned that they were powerless to escape its grasp.

Silvia no longer watched these cycles with despair. She had once believed in the necessity of opposition, of the tireless battle against injustice, but she had seen too much of how resistance, when framed solely as struggle, too often became another form of servitude. Instead, she had built a life beyond the reach of those forces, one not defined by resistance but by creation, by presence, by the quiet act of living truthfully.

But this was not a lesson of retreat. It was not a call to turn away from the world, nor to abandon the fight for something better. It was, rather, an acknowledgment that the tools of the past, the centralized institutions, the rigid ideological doctrines, the reliance on hierarchical power, were no longer the only means by which people could carve out spaces of freedom.

The world had changed. And for those who sought their own paths, those unwilling to be swallowed by the endless churn of institutions or crushed under the weight of the same cycles of control, new possibilities had emerged.

Silvia had once sought meaning in texts, in ancient philosophies, in movements shaped by the hands of history.

But now she saw that the very means by which people could free themselves were shifting. The great thinkers of the past had shaped the revolutions of their time through books and discourse; now, new forms of expression had taken their place, decentralized networks, encrypted communications, digital art, alternative economies, and tools that allowed ideas to escape the grip of corporate and political control.

The printing press had once been the great disruptor. Now, there were technologies that allowed for the free exchange of thought beyond borders and censorship. There were AI-driven creations, tools that democratized knowledge, breaking the hold of gatekeepers who had long dictated what could be learned and who could learn it. There were open-source communities, decentralized forums where knowledge was shared, refined, and built upon without the oversight of institutions hungry for control. There were currencies outside the reach of banks, wealth stored in ways that did not depend on the approval of governments or financiers. There were tools that allowed artists to create, not as servants of commerce but as independent voices.

And yet, as with every revolution, the same dangers lurked. The old systems had not disappeared; they had adapted, repackaged themselves in the language of innovation while seeking new ways to consolidate power. The same hierarchies that once ruled empires now sought to rule algorithms. The same greed that had once built kingdoms now built corporate monopolies that profited from the illusion of freedom. Even the new tools of liberation could be turned against their users if wielded carelessly, if not understood for what they were.

Silvia knew this well. She had spent too many years watching revolutions become institutions, watching ideals become dogma. The lesson was not to abandon new possibilities, but to wield them wisely. Not to trust in any system, old or new, to deliver freedom, but to recognize that freedom must always be claimed, practiced, and defended.

As she sat in her garden, she imagined a future where people, like her, refused to be owned by systems, where they did not seek to take power but to step beyond its reach. A future where knowledge was freely exchanged, where creation did not depend on permission, where individuals could build lives outside the grasp of those who sought to control them.

She knew not everyone would choose this path. Many would continue the old fights, believing that change must come from within the very institutions that had resisted it for centuries. She did not fault them for this. Change came in many forms, and each person had to find their own way. But for those who sought something else, for those who were tired of trying to break a machine that only rebuilt itself, there was another way.

A life built, not on opposition, but on creation. Not on ideology, but on truth. Not on power, but on freedom.

Silvia had found that life. And she knew that others would find their own.

As the sun set, she whispered one final promise to herself, knowing that it would be kept, not because it was written in doctrine or law, but because it was lived, each day, in the quiet revolution of simply being free.

About EATMS Productions

What's happening to women now is not random. It's structural.

Policy, culture, technology, and power are moving in the same direction.

EATMS maps them clearly and shows how to respond.

This title is part of an ongoing body of work. All EATMS Productions titles, across all series, authors, and formats, are components of a single connected project.

Start here: EATMS System Primer — Free Bundle
https://eatms.gumroad.com/l/dyvzbw

For full catalog or inquiries: eatms.me

Free survival booklet + EATMS updates: email "EATMS" to eatms@pm.me

Please feel free to burn part or all of this book, safely, as an effigy.

www.ingramcontent.com/pod-product-compliance
Lightning Source LLC
LaVergne TN
LVHW051001080826
845145LV00009B/2391

* 9 7 8 1 9 6 6 0 1 4 9 5 9 *